# FOUL DEEDS IN
# ISLINGTON

# Foul Deeds in
# ISLINGTON

## John J Eddleston

First Published in Great Britain in 2010 by
Wharncliffe Local History
*an imprint of*
Pen and Sword Books Limited,
47 Church Street, Barnsley,
South Yorkshire. S70 2AS

**ISBN: 978 184563 127 7**

A CIP catalogue record of this book is available from the
British Library.

Typeset in Plantin and Benguiat by
S L Menzies-Earl

Printed in the UK by the MPG Books Group


*Pen & Sword Books Ltd incorporates the imprints of*
Pen & Sword Aviation, Pen & Sword Maritime,
Pen & Sword Military, Wharncliffe Local History, Pen & Sword
Select, Pen & Sword Military Classics, Leo Cooper, Remember
When, Seaforth Publishing and Frontline Publishing

*For a complete list of Pen & Sword titles please contact:*
PEN & SWORD BOOKS LIMITED
47 Church Street, Barnsley, South Yorkshire, S70 2AS, England.
E-mail: enquiries@pen-and-sword.co.uk
Website: www.pen-and-sword.co.uk

# Contents

# Introduction

The district of Islington has long had a somewhat Bohemian reputation and is, nowadays, one of the more fashionable areas of the city. Islington, however, has a darker side.

This book contains details of some fifty men and women who faced a charge of murder, for crimes within Islington. Some of these were crimes of desperation and rage, such as the murder of the writer Joe Orton by his lover, Kenneth Halliwell; a sad story of a man eclipsed by his more famous partner, or the slashing of James Frederick Robinson by Nicky Xanaris, in a street fight. There are, however, also the cold-blooded killers who took the lives of others for more sinister reasons.

There is the story of George Chapman, a man said by some to be the infamous Jack the Ripper. That is almost certainly nonsense, but it is true that he poisoned three women and watched them die slowly and painfully.

Yet such evil is not limited to the male of the species. The story of Celestina Somner is also told in these pages; a woman who calmly took her own daughter into a cellar, cut her throat, and then encouraged her to die, expressing impatience when the child did not die quickly enough.

*Foul Deeds in Islington* tells the stories of wives, killed by their husbands, men killed in drunken fights, children killed by those they should have been able to trust, and of deaths that remain unsolved to this day. Each of those stories is the story of someone's life and death; lives cut short for no other reason than drunkenness, carelessness or anger. It also tells the stories of those who spent their final days in the condemned cell of one of London's prisons, waiting for the hangman to come and end their suffering. Every one of the chapters signals the death of one or more persons, sometimes in the most brutal of fashions.

The streets of Islington today may well be places to aspire to, but some of those same streets hold tales of violent, brutish death, by the knife, the cosh, the gun, the blunt instrument, the bottle of deadly poison, and the unforgiving judicial rope.

Those dark tales are told within the pages of this book.

# Acknowledgements

I would like to offer my thanks to my wife, Yvonne, who proof-read the entire book before submission, helped with the original research, and assisted with suggestions for improvements in many of the chapters.

My thanks must also go to the staff of The National Archives at Kew. They always provide a first-class, professional service, and it is always a pleasure to work there.

Finally, I must thank Alison Spence, an archivist at the Cornwall Record Office, for her assistance with the research on George Nicholls Simmons, for the chapter on William Henry Clarke.

# Sources

All references are from The National Archives (formerly Public Record Office, Kew):

HO 45/9315/15372, Lydia Venables; HO 144/235/A51321, Thomas Neal; CRIM 1/43/10, Alfred Chipperfield; HO 144/266/A57652, Alfred Chipperfield; CRIM 1/84, George Chapman; CRIM 1/97/4, Albert Bridgeman; CRIM 1/108/4, Walter Fensham; HO 144/15375, Walter Fensham; PCOM 9/734, Walter Fensham; CRIM 1/293, Arthur Robert Canham; HO 144/20627, Arthur Robert Canham; MEPO 3/1608, Arthur Robert Canham; CRIM 1/940, Frederick Murphy; DPP 2/463, Frederick Murphy; HO 144/20658, Frederick Murphy; HO 144/20659, Frederick Murphy; MEPO 3/874, Frederick Murphy; MEPO 3/1647, Frederick Murphy; CRIM 1/1831, Harry Morley; HO 45/22559, Harry Morley; CRIM 1/2577, Nicky Xinaris; PCOM 9/2201, Nicky Xinaris; CRIM 1/3147, Ronald Henry Marwood; HO 291/242, Ronald Henry Marwood; HO 291/243, Ronald Henry Marwood; PCOM 9/2095, Ronald Henry Marwood; CRIM 1/3946, John Patrick Quinlan

# Chapter 1

# Henry Asher
# 1836

On the late afternoon of Wednesday 2 March 1836, between 5.00pm and 5.30pm, seven-year-old Edward Soall was playing, by himself, close to the gutter at the edge of the pavement, at the top end of Park Street, (now renamed Islington Park Street).

Suddenly, a dray turned into Park Street and travelled, at some speed, on the wrong side of the road. Edward Soall had his back to the dray, and did not see how close it was to him. When the dray had passed by, the broken body of Edward Soall was left lying half on the pavement, with his legs in the gutter. He was unconscious, and obviously very badly injured.

A gentleman named Frederick Cooper saw the accident, and ran to the child's aid. Lifting him gently, Cooper carried Edward to the surgery of William Burroughs, at 1 Park Street. The unfortunate child died there, fifteen minutes later. During the time that Edward was being attended to by the doctor, the driver of the dray was brought in, by others who had seen the tragedy. The man, Henry Asher, was arrested and charged with manslaughter.

Henry Asher faced his trial on 4 April 1836. The first witness was Frederick Cooper, the man who had taken the stricken child to the doctor's surgery.

Cooper told the court that he had seen that Edward Soall had been on the right-hand side of the street, when the dray turned into Park Street, travelling at a very fast pace. The driver, Henry Asher, was sitting on the cross-bar, on the left side of the dray and did not appear to be in command of the horse. In effect, the animal was running wild, and bore off towards the right side of the street, and Asher had apparently been powerless to prevent it. Cooper could not tell if it had been the horse, or the dray itself, which struck the boy, but he ran over to him as soon as he saw the boy lying stricken on the pavement. After carrying Edward to the doctor's, Cooper waited to see how he was, and was present when the boy died. He was also present when Cooper was brought into the surgery, and Dr Burroughs told him that he had just killed a child.

Henry Marsh, the next witness, was at the bottom of Park Street, and saw the dray when it turned into it. He also believed that the contraption was not under the control of the driver, and travelling far too fast. Marsh did not see the accident itself, but did notice Edward lying in the street after the dray had passed.

Thomas Godbold, a baker, lived in Park Street, almost opposite to where Edward Soall was hit. After the accident he had called out to Asher to stop, but he seemed not to hear and carried on down the street. Godbold followed the carriage and saw it turn into Cross Street. It was there that he spoke to the driver, and told him that he had just knocked a child down in Park Street. At first, Asher refused to go back to the scene, but eventually he agreed to go. Godbold ended his evidence by stating that, in his opinion, Asher was under the influence of drink at the time.

Dr William Burroughs confirmed that Edward Soall had been unconscious when he was brought into the surgery by Frederick Cooper. He died within fifteen minutes and, the following day, Dr Burroughs made a post-mortem examination. The boy had two fractured ribs on the right side. One rib had punctured the right lung and this had caused some twelve ounces of blood to drain into the chest cavity. Dr Burroughs believed that, severe though the injuries were, they would have been even worse if the wheel of the dray had run over the boy. In his opinion, the injury had been caused by a blow from the horse's hooves, striking Edward in his back and pushing him violently to the ground.

At about the same time as Edward Soall died, Henry Asher was brought into the surgery. Dr Burroughs asked him his name, and Asher replied that his name was of no consequence and he would not reveal it. Dr Burroughs then asked Asher if the dray were his own, and he confirmed that it was. Burroughs found this unlikely and demanded to know who his master was. Again, Asher refused to give out any information. It as then that the doctor sent for the police.

Constable William Stotter was the officer who arrived at the surgery and took charge of Asher. Stotter also believed that Asher was tipsy, but despite that, and the fact that he had just run over a small boy, Asher was allowed to drive his dray to the police station, where he was charged with manslaughter.

In his own defence, forty-one-year-old Henry Asher could only say: 'I am very sorry for what has occurred, but I am innocent of it. I knew nothing of it at all until I was stopped and went back. I did not refuse to go back. but went quietly, and made every offer of recompense that I could.'

It was not enough to sway the jury who found Asher guilty of manslaughter. He was then sentenced to the rather lenient total of six months in jail.

# Chapter 2

# William Madden
## 1838

Some time in January 1838, nineteen-year-old William Madden, a costermonger, was involved in a violent assault on his own brother. One of the main witnesses against Madden, at the later court hearing, was James Wallis. It was his evidence that largely convicted Madden who, because he could not post bail, was then sent to prison. As he was taken down to the cells, Madden swore that he would have his revenge upon Wallis.

William Madden was released from prison on Wednesday 7 February and immediately decided to seek retribution against the man, who he believed was responsible for his spell in jail. He spent the rest of that day searching for Wallis but did not find him until the early evening.

It was around 5.00pm, as Ann Whittington walked along Lower Road, Islington, and as she approached the corner of Britannia Row, she saw a two men squaring up to each other. One of them, a man she would later identify as William Madden, struck the other man three or four times around the head. This second man, later shown to be James Wallis, fell to the ground, insensible. This assault was also seen by William Payne, a hairdresser, of 19 Lower Road, and a friend of Wallis.

James Wallis could not be roused so Payne, and a number of other men, carried him to the surgery of Dr Robert Martin, at 10 Cross Street. Dr Martin made a careful examination, but could find no marks of violence, apart from a little black mark underneath Wallis's left ear, and a few minor scratches on his face. Dr Martin could not, however, rouse his patient and, later that same evening, James Wallis died. William Madden now found himself facing a murder charge.

The inquest on the dead man opened two days later, on 9 February, at the *King's Head* public house, also on Lower Road. The proceedings began with a brief history of the previous trouble between Madden and Wallis. Madden had struck his brother and then been charged with assault at the Hatton Garden police station. After Wallis had given evidence that Madden was the instigator of the trouble, he was sent to prison and, as he was taken down, Madden was heard to say that he would 'do for' Wallis just as soon as he regained his freedom.

John Lea was an acquaintance of both men involved in this case. Some three weeks before the attack upon Wallis, Lea had gone to visit Madden, who was held in the Clerkenwell prison. Madden was obviously still bearing a grudge against both his brother and Wallis, for he asked Lea to deliver a message to both of them. The gist of that message was that he would give them both a sound thrashing when he got out of jail. He also repeated his threat that he would do for Wallis.

Lea did not see the attack upon Wallis on 7 February, but some fifteen minutes later, at around 5.15pm, he saw Madden in Ward's Place. Madden appeared to be very happy with himself, and when Lea asked him why he was so pleased, Madden replied that he had, 'cooked Wallis's potatoes for him', a rather curious way of saying that he had settled the score between them.

Having heard all the evidence against Madden, the inquest jury returned a verdict of manslaughter against Madden and he was sent to face his trial on that charge. That trial took place on 26 February, when further evidence was given as to the precise cause of James Wallis's death.

Dr Martin had, by this time, performed a post-mortem on the dead man and he reported the rupture of a large blood vessel in the neck. In his opinion, the three or four blows to the neck area had damaged the carotid artery, causing a suffusion of blood into that area. This was the direct cause of death.

William Payne was a close friend of James Wallis and had been with him at the time of the attack. He told the court that he and Wallis had been walking peacefully down Lower Road, when

Madden suddenly appeared from around a corner. Without warning, and certainly without any provocation, Madden then struck Wallis three or four hard blows to the left of his neck. Wallis had not retaliated but had merely said: 'Come into the fields and I will fight you.' Almost as soon as he had spoken those words, he collapsed unconscious to the floor.

Henry Hayes was another friend of Wallis and he was with him in Lower Road when the attack took place. Hayes was one of the men who helped William Payne carry the injured man to the doctor's surgery.

There could be little doubt that the blows inflicted by Madden were the direct cause of James Wallis's death and the jury duly returned a guilty verdict. William Madden, who had actively sought revenge, and taken a man's life in the process, was then given a sentence of six months in prison.

# Chapter 3

# Richard Gould
## 1840

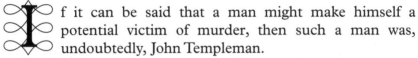

I f it can be said that a man might make himself a potential victim of murder, then such a man was, undoubtedly, John Templeman.

John lived in an isolated cottage, called Lincoln Cottage, in Pocock's Fields, a lonely patch of land at the rear of Liverpool Road, which was adjacent to Barnsbury Park, Islington. There were a few cottages in that area, but all were detached and separated from the neighbouring houses. Added to that, John Templeman, whose income came solely from the rents of properties he owned, was an elderly gentleman, and often boasted of the money he had. Those boasts and John's circumstances, soon became well known in the Islington area.

On Monday 16 March 1840, John travelled to Somer's Town to collect his rents. That routine, too, was well known. That afternoon, John sent for Mary Ann Thornton, a woman who lived in a cottage opposite, and who he employed as a charwoman. John explained that he wished to write some letters, and asked Mary if she would get him some writing paper, and bring it when she called the next day.

On Tuesday 17 March, Mary Thornton sent her daughter, Elizabeth, to John's cottage at 8.30am, with the writing paper. Elizabeth knocked at the door, but received no answer. Thinking that Mr Templeman might still be in bed, though he was normally an early riser, Elizabeth went to look in at the bedroom window. There was a shutter drawn down, so Elizabeth could see nothing of the room inside. She then went to look through the sitting-room window, but still saw nothing. Elizabeth ran home to tell her mother that Mr Templeman wasn't answering his door.

Mary went across to Lincoln Cottage, to investigate for herself. She knocked on the door first, but again there was no reply. Going to the bedroom window, Mary looked more carefully than her daughter had done, and managed to catch a glimpse of the room, through a small gap in the shutter. She saw John Templeman lying on the floor, close to his bed.

It might well have been expected that Mary Thornton should have, immediately, reported this discovery to the police, but she did not do so. Instead, she went home and waited for her son-in-law, Francis Capriani, who was due to arrive later that morning. He appeared at 11.00am but, having been told that Mr Templeman was lying on the floor of his cottage, the police were still not informed. Instead, a message was sent to John Templeman's grandson, Mr Herbert Coates Templeman, a solicitor who practised in Cavendish Square. It was he, who finally informed the police, that his grandfather was in need of assistance.

No less than three police officers attended at Lincoln Cottage, at around 11.20am. Constable William Kear, Sergeant John Collins and Inspector James Miller arrived with two doctors: Dr Edward Roe and Dr Alfred Lord. They gained entry to the cottage, and found that John Templeman was dead. There were several wounds on the back of his head, and his forehead had been completely smashed in. So fierce had the attack upon him been, that three teeth had been knocked out and were found on the bedroom carpet near his body. They also determined that the most likely time of death was in the early hours of that morning.

The motive for the crime had obviously been one of robbery. A money-drawer had been forced open, and was now empty. As for the method of entry, the parlour window had been broken, for some time, and the hole had been stuffed with paper. Anyone could simply remove that paper, reach in and unfasten the window catch.

Largely because of their somewhat strange behaviour in not reporting this matter immediately to the authorities, both Mary Thornton and Francis Cipriani were taken to the police station, for further questioning. Mary was soon released, but Francis remained in custody overnight. He appeared before the magistrates the following morning, Wednesday 18 March, and explained that he lived with Mary Thornton and was a night-watchman, at the Sadler's Wells Theatre. Francis went on to admit that he occasionally did some gardening work for Mr Templeman, and indeed had done some on Monday 16 March, for which he had been paid seven shillings. Finally, Francis was able to prove that he had been at the theatre until 9.00am, on the Tuesday, and so was at work at the time the crime was committed. He was then released from custody.

There had, however, been further developments in the meantime. About one year before, Mary Anne Allen, who lived at Wilson's Cottage in Pocock's Fields, had had a lodger named Richard Gould. Just a few days before the murder of John Templeman, Gould had returned to her house, and asked Mary if she would let him lodge with her again. As part of the routine police enquiries all the neighbouring cottages had been visited and searched, and when police examined this particular house, they found £5 in cash, mostly silver, and some bloodstained clothing. Gould was arrested on suspicion, as were Mary Ann Jarvis, a friend of Gould, who had called on him a number of times prior to the murder, and her husband, John. Eventually, the latter were both released without charge, but the evidence against Gould was considered strong enough to send him for trial.

Richard Gould appeared at the Old Bailey on 6 April, before Mr Justice Littledale. Gould's defence lay in the hands of Mr Chambers, assisted by Mr Caarlen, whilst the prosecution case was detailed by Mr Jones, who was assisted by Mr Ballantine.

Constable William Kear gave details of what he had found upon entering Lincoln Cottage, on the morning of Tuesday 17 March. Kear had gained entrance through the sitting-room window, the same method most probably used by the killer. Kear then went to the front door and unlocked it, so that the others could gain access.

John Templeman lay on his back, close to his bed, his hands tied in front of him with a cord. There was a stocking, which was covering his eyes, and tied at the back of his head. He wore nothing but a night-shirt. Constable Kear searched the premises and found two drawers had been forced open. The wood was splintered, suggesting that a tool such as a chisel had been used. Later, Kear found the three teeth, all lying in separate pools of blood.

Dr Edward Roe was the next witness, and he stated that Templeman had certainly fought for his life. In Dr Roe's opinion, the first blow had been one to the left temple, with a heavy blunt object such as a piece of wood, or a club of some kind. Another blow had fractured the jaw, and there was also a wound to the nose, most probably caused by a severe kick to the face. Finally, there were two wounds on the back of the head, caused by some sort of sharp instrument, such as a chisel.

Dr Alfred Lord, who had also visited the scene of the crime, and later assisted Dr Roe in the post-mortem, confirmed the findings of the previous witness, and added that the first blow, the one to the temple, was of itself sufficient to cause death. It would certainly have rendered the victim unconscious immediately.

Sergeant John Collins had also searched the premises and found a small, mahogany cash box, which had been forced open. It only contained a few personal papers, and the key to this box was later found, in a pair of John Templeman's trousers. In the same pocket, Collins found the only cash left on the premises, three sixpenny pieces.

The fact that John Templeman should have had far more than the one shilling and sixpence found in his property, was demonstrated by the next few witnesses. Jane Lovett was one of Templeman's tenants, and she confirmed that she had paid him £3 on Monday 16 March. In amongst that amount, there was at least five half-crowns and one sovereign. The rest had been in smaller silver, such as shillings and sixpences.

Hannah Morgan, another tenant, said that she had also paid Mr Templeman £3. This consisted of fourteen half-crowns and twenty-five shillings. The testimony of both of these witnesses meant that John Templeman should have had at least £6 in cash in his home, and that £5 of that amount should have been in silver coins.

John Mustow lived in the cottage at the back of Mr Templeman's, and he testified that he had often seen Gould, the prisoner, in the area. He knew Gould as a potman. at the *Barnsbury Castle* public house, and he used to deliver beer to the houses in Pocock's Fields. Mustow was also able to confirm that Mr Templeman had often boasted of how much money he had.

Henry Wright was a potman at the *Duchess of Kent*, and knew Gould as a customer there. On either 12 or 13 March, Wright could not be sure which, Gould was in the pub and only had one penny in cash. Wright had taken pity on him and stood him a pint of porter. Later, as they talked together, Gould mentioned that he knew an old man who had plenty of money, which he kept in a drawer in his house. Asked where this house was, Gould had replied: 'Oh, not far.'

John Richard Johnson had known Gould for somewhere between four and five years. On Friday 13 March, Johnson had seen Gould, who asked him if he could see Jem, a man who worked for Johnson, so that he could ask him where he might get a screw, which was a slang term for a lock-pick. Johnson, quite naturally, asked why he wanted such a thing, and Gould had replied that he knew of an old man, who lived in a lonely cottage, and had money hidden away.

The Jem that Johnson had referred to was James Rogers, and he had spoken to Gould later on 13 March. Gould had asked him for a screw and a dark lantern, but Johnson had replied that he might as well ask him for a £500 note, as he had no intention of helping him in any way.

Charles Allen was the husband of Mary Anne, who lived at Wilson's Cottage, and he testified that Gould had lodged with them a number of times. He had last gone to stay there about a week before Mr Templeman was murdered. Charles knew that on 13 March, Gould had had no money, as he was unable to pay for any breakfast. Gould did say, however, that he would have some money at the weekend.

Another witness to Gould having no money, before the

murder, was Robert King. On the night of Monday 16 March, he had been in the *Rainbow* public house on Liverpool Road. Gould was also there, playing skittles in the yard. At one stage he mentioned, to King, that he only had a halfpenny in his pocket.

Also in the Rainbow, was King's wife, Mary Elizabeth. She noticed, at closing time, that Gould had something in his right-hand coat pocket. The object appeared to be quite long, and was thicker at one end. As all the people left the beerhouse, Mary noticed that Gould walked off in the direction of Lincoln Cottage.

Inspector James Miller had gone to search Gould's lodgings, and found nine shilling coins in his jacket pocket. He had also found a bloodstained waistcoat. Later, when the privy of the house was searched, Miller found a stocking hidden between the rafters and the roof. The stocking was quite heavy, and when Miller looked inside he found nineteen half-crowns, forty-eight shillings and seven sixpences, making a total of £4 19s.

The jury, it seems, did not see the significance, of the basic facts in this case. Gould had been without money in the days leading up to the murders, yet had money on him when he was arrested. More money was found hidden in the outhouse, at his lodgings, money that his landlord and landlady denied having hid there. Gould had also told more than one person that he intended getting some money from an old man who lived in an isolated cottage, and bloodstained clothing had been found in his room. Even more telling, perhaps, was that the number of half-crowns paid to Mr Templeman by his two tenants, was nineteen; precisely the number found in the hidden stocking.

Despite all this, the jury did not think that they had enough evidence to convict, and returned a not guilty verdict. Gould walked from court a free man, quite possibly responsible for a violent robbery and a most brutal murder.

# Chapter 4

# Thomas Cooper
## 1842

In the early months of 1842, there had been a number of robberies in the area of Hornsey Wood and north Islington. A man had been walking up to people, brandish a pistol, and like some fictional highwayman had demanded, 'Your money or your life.' Cash, watches and gold chains had been taken and, as a result, police officers in that area had been furnished with a basic description, and told to be on the look-out for anyone behaving suspiciously.

On Friday 5 May 1842, Constable Charles Moss was patrolling his beat in Hornsey, when he saw a man walking towards him, who fitted the description of the armed robber. As the man passed Moss, the officer turned and watched him go into a house nearby. Moss decided he had mistaken the man, and he hadn't been the robber after all, and so continued on his beat. He had only gone a few more steps, when another man, walking towards him, ran over to the opposite side of the road, jumped over a hedge, and vanished into a field.

Constable Moss thought that such behaviour warranted further investigation, so climbed over a stile and entered the field himself. For a few moments, he failed to see the man but then, turning to his left, Moss saw the man crouching down on the grass, and in front of him, on the ground, were two pistols.

Moss demanded to know what the man was doing. He replied: 'Nothing in particular.' Moss was far from satisfied, and said that if he was not able to give a better account of himself, he would have to come to the police station, and explain himself there. At that, the man leapt to his feet, picking up the pistols as he did, and brandishing one in each hand towards Moss.

Constable Moss bravely took a step forward, and the man

fired the pistol in his right hand. A searing pain struck Moss in his left arm, just above the elbow. Still Moss moved forward, whereupon the armed man pulled the trigger of the other pistol, but it failed to go off. Moss now rushed at his man and was rewarded with a blow to the head from the pistol, which had failed to discharge. By now, Moss had started to weaken somewhat, due to the wound in his arm, and had to let his assailant go. The man quickly ran off, with the injured Moss in pursuit.

As the two men ran over the fields, heading down towards north Islington, Moss shouted for help, from the people who he passed. Some of those men who heard his cries, joined in with the chase. Then, due largely to the loss of blood, Constable Moss fell to the ground. He would later spend weeks in hospital, before finally making a full recovery.

James Mallett was another constable on duty near Hornsey Wood, when he heard the sound of a shot. Going to investigate, he saw Moss, and other men, chasing a man who had a pistol in each hand. By now, the gunman was running along Hornsey Road, and Mallett now joined in the chase. In all, the crowd followed the man for close on two miles, as he moved further and further south, into Islington.

When Constable Moss had fallen, in the field, John William Young, a waiter at the Hornsey Wood Tavern, had come to his aid. Seeing that the officer was not in danger of dying, he too joined in the chase and, at one point, passed another constable, who he told that a brother officer had been shot. This constable, Timothy Daly, also joined in the chase, leaving Moss to wait for medical aid to arrive.

In due course, the gunman found himself out of breath, and trapped in a small cul-de-sac lane off Highbury Park. He turned, his back to a wooden fence, and faced the mob of people who were still pursuing him. There were, perhaps, twenty people in that mob, including Constable Daly, and a baker named Charles Mott.

The crowd of people formed a semi-circle around the gunman and Daly, being the only uniformed officer there at the time, stepped forward to take charge of the man. The pistols were raised again but, as Daly stepped forward he commented that he did not believe they were loaded. The gunman said that they were, and that he would be happy to let the officer have the contents of them. Then, as the gunman had his eyes fixed upon Daly, Charles Mott saw his chance.

Rushing forward to seize the fugitive, Mott managed to lose his footing, and slipped down as he grabbed the man's waist. A shot rang out, and Mott was wounded in the shoulder. Constable Daly had also moved forward, and a second shot hit him in the head. His guns now useless, as they would need to be reloaded, the gunman dropped them, and reached into his jacket pocket. Someone shouted that he had a large knife, whereupon the crowd leapt upon him and subdued him. The weapons were all confiscated, and the prisoner then marched to the police station. It was there that he identified himself as twenty-three-year-old Thomas Cooper, of 1 Rawstorne Street, Clerkenwell.

Later that same day, Inspector George Thatcher informed Cooper, that he would be charged with the murder of Constable Timothy Daly. An incredulous Cooper asked: 'Is he dead then?' When that was confirmed, George Cooper went very pale, and seemed as if he were about to faint.

Cooper's trial for murder took place on 13 June 1842, at the Old Bailey. He pleaded not guilty to murder, his defence team claiming that he was insane at the time of the shooting.

After Constable Moss and Constable Mallett had given their testimony, John Young, the waiter, was called to the stand. He had been one of the group of men, who had been gathered around Cooper at the time of the shooting. Young had heard Daly say that he didn't believe the pistols were loaded, two or three times, and each time Cooper had replied that they were. Young had been one of those who seized hold of Cooper, once Daly had been shot.

Other witnesses to the shooting, who formed part of the crowd, were John William Howard, Stephen Turnbull, William Smith, Thomas Grover, James Wheeler and Erasmus Simmons. Turnbull testified that he was the man who wrestled the knife from Cooper, after the pistols had been discarded. Thomas

Grover said that after Mott had been shot, Cooper seemed to take deliberate aim at Constable Daly, and Simmonds said that he had picked up the two pistols, after Cooper had discarded them. All the three weapons were then handed to Wheeler, who carried them to the police station.

The final witness, after those who had surrounded Cooper in Highbury Park, was Charles Mott, who told of the wound he had suffered, when he tried to rush Cooper. He had been in the hospital ever since, and was still not fit to return to work.

For the defence, witnesses were called, to show that Cooper was not a sane person. The first of these was his mother, Isabella, who testified that her son had been very ill when he was a very young child. Ever since that time, he had been different. He was very restless and hardly slept at night. He also seemed to be oblivious to pain. On one occasion, when he was a child of twelve, a pan of steaming hot broth had been spilled on his arm. So bad was the resulting scald that Cooper's flesh came away when his shirt was removed. He didn't flinch once, and said that it just didn't bother him. He never seemed to grow up, and still played games where he said he was either King Richard or Dick Turpin. He also collected guns, and would rather spend his money on weapons, than food.

Hannah Southall had once lodged with the Coopers, and she testified that Thomas had always been strange in his behaviour. Many times he had said he was tired of life, and once he had taken laudanum, and his mother had been forced to administer castor oil to him.

The final witness was Dr Gilbert McMurdo, the surgeon at Newgate prison. He was called to counter any possibility of Cooper escaping with a verdict of insanity. He had had the prisoner under close observation, ever since he had been admitted to Newgate, and testified that he saw no signs of Cooper having an unsound mind.

With all the witnesses to the shooting, the jury had little difficulty in returning a guilty verdict, whereupon Cooper was sentenced to death. There was no reprieve and, on 4 July 1842, Thomas Cooper was hanged outside Newgate prison.

# Chapter 5

# Other Crimes
## 1800-1850

### (1) William Field, 1807

On 16 August 1807, William Field was enjoying a quiet drink in the *Clown* public house at Islington, when he saw something which he strongly objected to.

Also in the bar, was James Warwick, a man who was known as something of a bully, and on this particular day, he had decided to annoy an elderly man. Not one to simply let this pass, Field went over, and suggested to Warwick, that he sit down and behave himself.

The old man left soon afterwards and, once he had gone, Field told Warwick that he should be ashamed of himself, for treating an elderly man in such a way. Warwick now turned his attention to Field, and told him that he would split his nose. He then offered to fight him, for money, and suggested a side bet of £10.

Anxious not to get involved any further, Field said he had no money, whereupon Warwick said that he would reduce the wager to just £1. When Field still refused to fight, Warwick called him and his friends beggars. It was at that point, that one of Field's friends put £1 down. The fight was on.

The two men fought for over an hour, until those who had been in Warwick's company saw that he was clearly getting the worst of it, and announced that he would fight no more. The fight ended, but Warwick appeared to have been quite badly injured. He was taken to hospital and died later the same day.

Charged with manslaughter, William Field appeared in court on 16 September. The jury, having heard that Warwick had been the one to instigate the fight, decided that Field was not guilty in any way, and he walked from court a free man.

### (2) Joseph Clare, 1818

It was an argument about nothing really. On the afternoon of 23 December 1817, Joseph Clare was drinking in the *Wheatsheaf* public house in Islington. He had spent most of the day sitting in one particular chair, by the roaring fire but, at around 2.30pm, he got up for a few minutes, to relieve himself. When he returned, he found a man named Gregory Pridden sitting in his seat.

Clare began by pointing out that Pridden had taken his seat. Pridden replied that no seat was reserved, it had been empty when he sat down in it, and he now had no intention of vacating it. Clare then told him that if he did not move instantly, he would drag him from the chair. The discussion became a full-blown argument, and Clare then threw himself upon Pridden and the two men rolled onto the floor.

After a short fight, Clare regained his coveted seat and Pridden left the public house altogether. This was not, however, the end of the matter, for just a few minutes later, Pridden was back and asking to fight again. Another brief struggle followed, during which, Pridden hit his head against a heavy table leg.

Over the next few days, Pridden complained to his wife, Eliza, that he was suffering from a very bad headache. His condition did not improve and, three days later, on 26 December, he died. Joseph Clare now found himself under arrest, and charged with manslaughter.

Clare's trial took place on 14 January 1818. Various witnesses were called, including Thomas Cuthbert, and William Carter, both of whom had been in the *Wheatsheaf* on 23 December. Both testified that Pridden had been sitting opposite to Clare and, when the latter went to the toilet, Pridden had stolen his seat. The fight had been Pridden's fault, and the blow to his head had been a pure accident.

The final witness was Dr William Wilton, who had taken care of Pridden in the last three days of his life. Whilst it was true that he had sustained a fractured rib, Pridden had other medical problems, including a disease of the viscera and a diseased liver and spleen. His lungs were also heavily congested, and it was likely that he would not have lived long under any circumstances. The fight, and the blow which he had received from the table, might well have hastened his death, but could not be said to be the direct cause.

With the testimony of those witnesses, the jury decided that Pridden's death had been accidental and Joseph Clare was in no way responsible. He walked from court a free man.

## (3) John Turner, Edward Jones and John Smith, 1823

On the morning of Sunday 26 October 1823, at around 7.00am, Thomas Carroll called upon his friend, Benjamin Sarson, at his home in Grub Street, and asked him to accompany him to the *Rosemary Branch* public house, in Islington. Carroll, it appeared, had agreed to take part in a prize fight.

At the Rosemary Branch, Carroll and Sarson met up with three men, John Turner, Edward Jones and John Smith. The fight was to take place between Carroll and Turner, with various spectators taking side bets on the outcome.

Turner handed a sovereign over to a man named George Owen, who was to act as the unofficial bookmaker. Another man, named Hurd, also handed over twenty shillings, as a bet on Turner. Once all the bets were placed, the two protagonists shook hands, in a most friendly manner, and Carroll even said to his opponent: 'We will bear no animosity after the fight is over, but be good friends.'

Turner and Carroll fought for a full fifty minutes, with Carroll, the taller of the two men, seemingly getting the better of Turner. Then, suddenly, Turner landed a blow under Carroll's ear, which caused him to fall to the ground. An unconscious Carroll was then carried to his father's house nearby but, over the next few weeks, his condition grew steadily worse. Unfortunately, the family did not call for the surgeon until a month had passed.

Dr Septimus Read attended Carroll on the morning of 27 November. He found his patient still unconscious. Despite Dr Read's attempts to revive Carroll, the man died later that same day. The matter was reported to the police, who arrested Turner for striking the fatal blow, and the other two, Jones and Smith, for encouraging the fight. All three were charged with manslaughter.

The trial of the three men took place on 3 December. Various witnesses stated that the fight had been a fair one, and that Jones had even tried to stop it at one stage. Other men had also encouraged the two men to stop fighting, and whilst Turner had agreed, Carroll had refused, and said he would fight on until he dropped.

Dr Read confirmed that the direct cause of death had been an effusion of blood to the head, produced by external violence, but the problem for the jury, was that this had been a fight agreed to by both parties; two of the defendants had been heard, suggesting that the fight should be stopped; and medical attention had not been sought for a full month. Under the circumstances, the jury ruled that all three prisoners were not guilty of killing Carroll and they were immediately discharged.

### (4) William Broadway, 1827

William and his brother, John, lived with their mother in Brittania Row, Islington. The brothers were always very affectionate towards each other, and rarely argued.

On Sunday 29 April 1827, William noticed, at supper time, that his brother was not yet home. He told his mother, Mary Pheby, that he would go out and fetch John back. However, when he did return, William was alone.

A few minutes later, John Broadway came home. He was carrying a small can of beer, which he threw down onto the floor. Then, without a word of warning, he struck William, hard, in the face.

His anger up now, John shouted that he would do for William that night, and show him who was master in the house. William remained placid, and walked out of the house into the yard at the rear, saying that he would not fight with his brother. This did nothing to assuage John's anger, for he followed his brother and leapt upon him.

Knocking William to the floor, John sat astride him and struck out at his face repeatedly, forming a double fist with both hands clasped together. Still William did not retaliate. His mother, seeing all this, ran into the street and shouted for help. Her cries were heard by the local watchman, Thomas Sinfield.

Thomas dashed into the yard, and pulled John from William. He noticed that William's face was, by this time, very much swollen and bleeding rather badly. Now, for the first time, William too was angry. As Sinfield held John back, William picked up a small garden rake and struck his brother on the head.

It was nothing but a light blow, but William had, by accident rather than design, struck John with the pronged end. Three of those prongs inflicted minute wounds upon John's head.

Over the next few days, John complained that his head was sore, but refused to seek any medical attention until Saturday 5 May, when he finally agreed to the doctor being called out. Dr Robert Martin attended, and bled the patient, thinking that the wounds were not too serious. Unfortunately, John Broadway's condition did not improve, and he died on Monday 7 May.

Charged with murder, William Broadway appeared in court on 31 May. However, having heard that it had been John who had provoked William, and that he in turn had only retaliated with one small blow struck in anger, the jury decided that William had no case to answer, and found him not guilty.

## (5) Patrick Cadegan, 1834

Patrick Dunn was enjoying a pint of beer in the *Blakeney's Head* public house, at the top of Parcel's Court, Islington, on Sunday 17 August 1834. As he looked around the bar, he saw that a few of his neighbours were also there, including Timothy Brien.

A few minutes later, another neighbour, Patrick Cadegan, another regular at the *Blakeney's Head,* entered the pub, and ordered himself a drink. He was standing close to Timothy Brien, and the two men fell into conversation. Though Dunn could not be sure about what was said, the conversation soon turned into an argument, and Brien called Cadegan a bloody liar. The two men squared up to each other and, when Dunn stepped in between them, Brien offered to fight him instead.

Dunn could see that Brien was intoxicated and, thinking that it was better to avoid a confrontation, simply left the pub and walked home.

Brien, though, was not to be dissuaded. He followed Dunn to his house, at the other end of Parcel's Court and shouted: 'Come out and fight you bloody bastard.' When Dunn ignored this, Brien shouted: 'Come out you bloody rogue and fight me.'

By this time, a large crowd had gathered outside Patrick Dunn's house, and he saw no alternative, but to go out and try to quieten Brien. He managed to grab Brien and escort him back to his lodgings in George Yard, but once there, Brien managed to free himself, and tore Dunn's coat. A rather angry Dunn finally managed to half throw Brien into his lodgings, and close the door on him.

Even as this was happening, Patrick Cadegan, the original target of Brien's wrath, came down George Yard. By this time, Brien was leaning out of his window, on the ground floor, and Cadegan went up to him and said: 'Timothy Brien, what have you got to say to me?' but, before Brien could answer, Cadegan struck him, once, in the head. That blow was witnessed by Patrick Dunn, and another man who was walking down George Yard at the time, Thomas Costello. Unfortunately for Cadegan, within fifteen minutes of receiving that blow, Timothy Brien was dead.

Charged with manslaughter, Patrick Cadegan appeared in court on 4 September. Medical evidence was given by Dr Edward Cupples Dillon, who had been called to the scene, and later performed a post-mortem examination. He noted one small, black bruise beneath Brien's right ear, and upon opening the skull found a good deal of free blood around the brain. That single blow had ruptured a vein in Brien's head and caused him to bleed internally, leading to his rapid demise.

Found guilty of manslaughter, twenty-four-year-old Patrick Cadegan was sentenced to two years in prison.

## (6) John Norton, 1835

John Norton and his wife, Hannah, lived in George Yard,

Islington, but their relationship was not a happy one. Hannah was rather too fond of drink, and, whilst John also imbibed from time to time, he was largely a sober man. However, he also seemed to be rather fond of beating his wife.

On the afternoon of Sunday 22 August 1835, the long-suffering neighbours heard yet another argument, coming from the Norton's house. Ann McCarthy, who lived next door, heard raised voices and the sound of a scuffle. She simply drew down her blinds, to keep out the noise somewhat.

Bridget Welch was Hannah's daughter, from her first marriage, and lived further down George Yard. That evening, Bridget's brother, Thomas, brought their mother to Bridget's house. Hannah's jaw was hanging down and Hannah had great difficulty in speaking, but she did manage to say that John had struck her and broken her jaw. The family decided that Hannah needed medical treatment, and took her to the hospital.

Hannah was taken to the London Hospital. She was first seen by nurse Emma Parish, who confirmed that her jaw was broken. Hannah was then passed on to Dr James Duncan who treated her jaw, and a few minor bruises, which he had noticed. Hannah seemed to recover well, but on the late evening of Thursday 6 August, she suddenly became very restless. Her condition worsened and she became delirious. She died at noon on Friday 7 August and John Norton found himself facing a charge of manslaughter.

The trial took place on 17 August, when various witnesses told of the constant arguments between John and Hannah. More telling, perhaps, was the testimony of Dr Duncan.

In addition to detailing his treatment of Hannah, Dr Duncan said:

> I am not enabled to say what was the cause of her death. From the appearances, on dissection, I believe it was from a constitutional disturbance, occasioned by these blows, and the shattered state of her constitution. That is the only way we can account for her death; but I cannot say positively that the blows did cause her death. The anger and irritation of the moment, added to her bodily state, might

have caused her death. She might possibly have recovered, if she had been in a good state of health.

In short, Hannah's addiction to drink had greatly weakened her constitution but the doctor was unable to state with certainty, what the cause of death was, or if the actions of John Norton were responsible. Despite this, Norton was found guilty of manslaughter and sentenced to one year in prison.

### (7) George Rayner, 1839

On Monday 29 April 1834, an inquest opened at the *Pied Bull* public house, at Islington Green. The coroner, Mr Wakely, was investigating the death of twenty-five-year-old Elizabeth Foster, whose body had been recovered from the river on Wednesday 24 April. The proceedings were of great interest to a mechanic named George Rayner, for he had been arrested, and charged with murdering Elizabeth, before her throwing her lifeless body into the water.

Two witnesses, Frances Pursey, who was the sister of the landlord of *The Ship*, at Camden Street, and David Abrahams, the pot-boy, at that same establishment, both swore that they had seen the prisoner drinking with the deceased, on the night of Tuesday 23 April, and that they had left the public house together.

Dr Robert Henry Semple had performed the post-mortem on Elizabeth, and he said that there were no signs of violence upon her body. However, although there did not seem to be any of the usual signs of drowning, he was unable to state, with certainty, that the woman had not died as a result of being immersed in the water.

The evidence of Michael Nathan, a wholesale butcher, of 67 Aldgate High Street, was in direct contradiction to the two witnesses, Pursey and Abrahams, whose testimony had caused Rayner to be arrested.

Mr Nathan confirmed that Elizabeth had been in his service, for the past six months. She had remained at home all day on Tuesday 23 April, and he saw her retire to her bed at 11.30pm that night. When he came down the following morning, he had found that the premises were still locked up, with the door chain on. He had gone out for a couple of hours and, when he had returned, one of his workmen, Joseph Stebbins, said, they had seen Elizabeth leave the house at around 6.00am. Both Nathan and Stebbins also said that Elizabeth had been very down in her spirits over the past few weeks.

Summing up the evidence, the coroner asked if Rayner were still in custody. Told that he was, Mr Wakely said:

> I think there has been sufficient stated, to warrant his discharge. It is evident that the female, and the pot-boy at *The Ship*, were mistaken as to the identity of the deceased. There is no doubt that the deceased was found in the water, but how she came there, at present, there is no evidence to prove.

George Rayner was then discharged. He had been a very fortunate man indeed. There had been reports of the finding of a woman's body in the river, and those reports had been read by Michael Nathan, who had come forward, to positively identify Elizabeth, and prove that she was in Aldgate, at the time she was supposed to be drinking with Rayner. If it had not been for him, mistaken identity might well have hanged a completely innocent man.

### (8) Thomas Smith, 1840

On 15 June 1840, a trial opened at the Old Bailey. Thomas Smith, a drayman, was accused of unlawfully killing fifteen-month-old Emma Brooker, on Saturday 23 May.

There were a number of witnesses to the death of little Emma, in Liverpool Road, Islington. James Dolan was a resident of the street, and had been looking out of his window, when he saw the little girl standing on a piece of waste ground. As Smith's dray, travelling at a very slow speed, moved down Liverpool Road, Emma took a step forward and was caught by the near-side horse. This caused her to fall to the ground and the wheel of the dray then ran over her head.

John Howe was walking down Liverpool Road, between 7.00pm and 8.00pm, when he saw Emma fall and the wheel pass over her. He ran to the little girl, picked her up and took her to Dr Cooper's surgery nearby. Howe also testified, that as soon as the dray had run over the child, the driver stopped, and tried to assist in whatever way he could.

Constable Cornelius Savory was on duty in Liverpool Road, and had accompanied Howe, Smith and the child to the surgery. Once he had ascertained that the child was dead, he took Smith into custody, and later charged him with killing the child. At the time of his arrest, Smith was perfectly sober.

Fourteen-year-old Susannah Odell was playing on the waste ground, on the evening of 23 May. She saw Emma playing with her two sisters. The eldest of these had hold of Emma's hand, but at one stage she let go and Emma ran towards the road. Susannah believed that Emma had taken that last step into the road, to pick up a piece of paper, which was blowing along the street.

Dr Cooper confirmed that Emma was dead by the time she had been brought to the surgery. The cause of death was a fractured skull. The final witness, James Hooper, was one of the cashiers at Whitbread's Brewery, who employed Thomas Smith. Hooper confirmed that Smith had worked for the company for twenty-six years, and had an exemplary character.

It was clear that this entire affair was a tragic accident, and that Smith was in no way to blame for the child stepping out into the road. The jury found him not guilty and he walked from court a free man.

### (9) The Murder of Dr Crook, 1849

At around 6.00am, on the morning of 28 February 1849, Eli Deaver, on his way to work, walked into Dennis's Brick Field, on Caledonian Road, Islington. Immediately, his attention was attracted by the sound of a dog, barking furiously.

Turning to his left, Deaver saw a small black and white mongrel sitting at the feet of a man, lying on the cold and frozen ground. Going to investigate, Deaver saw that the man was lying in a pool of blood, a deep gash in his throat. As Deaver drew nearer, the dog growled and snapped at him, preventing him from getting too close.

Deaver ran for help, and soon the police were on the scene. The man in the field was quite tall, possibly around five feet, ten inches. He was aged somewhere between fifty and sixty, and had grey hair. He was obviously a gentleman, as his clothing was neat and expensive.

A search of the field revealed a number of clues. Though the body lay in a large pool of blood, there was another gory pool some twenty feet away. This suggested that the man had been attacked there, and then had managed to either crawl, or been carried, to where he was eventually found. As for a motive for this dastardly crime, that seemed to be indicated by the discovery of a man's purse five feet away. The purse was empty, except for a small key, indicating that robbery was the most likely motive for the attack.

The body was taken by the police to the vault of Islington Church where, later that same day, a positive identification was made. The dead man was Dr WH Crook, of 11 Bayham Street, Camden Town. No one was able to say what the doctor could possibly have been doing, in Islington.

The inquest on Dr Crook opened at the *Pied Bull* public house on 2 March. Little more could be stated with accuracy, apart from the fact that when he had been found, Dr Crook had been lying on his left side, with his hand underneath his body.

A workman, who lived in a hut in the field, said that he had heard a dog barking furiously, during the small hours of 28 February, which had been a particularly windy and blustery night. Beyond that, nothing else could give any clue, to either the time of the attack, or the name of the perpetrator. As a result, the jury had little choice but to return a verdict of murder by person or persons unknown.

# Chapter 6

# Jeremiah Tooley
## 1852

Mary Downes lived happily with her husband, Alexander, at 2 Suffolk Place, Suffolk Street, Islington. The area was a rather low-class one, and although many of the families there lived in abject poverty, there was, nevertheless, a strong sense of community, and the families all helped each other out whenever they could.

On Tuesday 7 December 1852, Mary was busy in her kitchen, cooking a joint of meat for her husband's dinner the next night. Alexander, meanwhile, stepped out into the communal yard at the back of the house, where he kept three dogs, so that he could feed them. It was then some time after 9.00pm.

Alexander had not been outside for very long, when Mary heard noises coming from the yard. It sounded like there was some sort of scuffle going on and, looking out of her window, Mary saw that her husband was struggling with another one of the lodgers at 2 Suffolk Place: Jeremiah Tooley. Even as Mary watched, Tooley took a razor out of his pocket and drew it across Alexander's throat. As Alexander slumped backwards, blood spurting from his neck, Tooley threw the bloody razor into a nearby dustbin.

Bravely, Mary ran out into the yard, shouting: 'Murder!' and grabbed hold of Tooley. Her screams and cries for assistance brought others to her aid, and Tooley was placed into custody. Alexander, meanwhile, was helped to the doctor's surgery but died within two minutes of his arrival.

Jeremiah Tooley appeared before the magistrates the next day, Wednesday 8 December. After Mary Downes had given her testimony, Ellen Godburn was called to the stand.

Ellen lived at 5 Suffolk Place, and she had been in her own

kitchen when she heard Mary Downes cry out from the yard. Looking out of her window, Ellen saw that Alexander Downes was supporting himself against a wall, bleeding badly from a wound in his throat. Mary Downes had, by now, run out into the yard and seized hold of Tooley, and was shouting for her neighbours to come to her aid. Ellen ran out and helped support Alexander, as he staggered with her, to the doctor's surgery.

Dennis Shea lived at 1 Suffolk Place, and he too heard the scream from Mary Downes. Dennis went into the yard and helped Mary to hold Tooley. Alexander, meanwhile, was being assisted by Ellen Godburn. Alexander tried to say something but the wound in his throat meant that he was unable to speak. Dennis then said to Tooley: 'You have murdered the man,' to which Tooley replied: 'Yes I have, and I would do it again.'

Mary Donovan was a servant girl, who lived with the Downes family. She saw her mistress struggling to hold Tooley in the yard, and Alexander bleeding from the throat. It was Mary who ran out into the street to find a policeman.

Constable Joseph Cotter was the officer Mary Donovan found. He immediately went to Suffolk Place. As he arrived, Ellen Godburn was just coming out of the house with Alexander Downes, to take him to the surgery. Constable Cotter took Tooley into custody, and escorted him to the police station. On the way, Tooley remarked that they had tried to poison him, that he was growing horns out of his head, and that Downes had not been satisfied with his own wife, but wanted his too. Since the incident, Constable Cotter had interviewed all the neighbours, but none could shed any light as to what the cause of the argument between the two men had been.

Dr William Butler practised medicine from his surgery at 19 Chapel Street, Clerkenwell. The injured man was brought to his surgery at around 10.00pm, but died within two minutes. Dr Butler noted a deep wound, starting below the left ear and going around the front of Alexander's throat. The carotid artery, the jugular vein, the trachea and the gullet had all been severed and at one part, the wound was through to the spine.

At the police station, Tooley had made a statement, which was then read out to the magistrates. It read:

> I have nothing at all to say, but I am out of my mind with them. You can have the doctor's opinion to say that state I am in, if you wish. I don't know what I am doing. She called me a cuckold, and said I was a cuckold by her own husband and that drove me mad. I don't know what I am doing.

Sent for trial, Tooley appeared at the Old Bailey, before Mr Justice Wightman, on 13 December. By now, Tooley's claim that the dead man had been having an affair with his wife, or that they had tried to poison him, were all found to be pure fantasy. There had been no reason whatsoever for him to take the life of Alexander Downes. As a result, only one witness was called at Tooley's trial.

Dr Gilbert McMurdo was the surgeon at Newgate prison and he informed the court that the prisoner was of unsound mind, and so was unfit to plead to the charge. As a result of that testimony, Jeremiah Tooley was ordered to be detained during Her Majesty's pleasure.

# Chapter 7

# Celestina Somner
# 1856

Rachel Munt was only fourteen years old and worked as a servant for Karl and Celestina Somner, at their house at 16 Linton Street, Islington. Rachel worked hard and slept in the kitchen each night, but was well looked after and was happy enough living with the family.

At around 10.00pm on the night of Saturday 16 February 1856, Celestina Somner told Rachel that she was going out. She approached Rachel in the kitchen and said: 'I am going into Murray Street, and shall be gone for about half an hour. I shall expect you to be in bed and asleep before I come back.'

Being a typical fourteen-year-old, Rachel did not, as her mistress had suggested, go straight to bed. Instead she stayed up, working on an apron she was sewing for herself. Then, some thirty minutes later, when Rachel heard the key turn in the front door, she simply climbed into bed, closed her eyes and pretended she was in a deep sleep.

It was certainly Rachel's mistress returning for Celestina called out: 'Are you in bed Rachel?' The girl did not reply and continued her pretence of being asleep as she heard Celestina go upstairs to her bedroom. She also heard her say, to someone she must have brought home with her: 'Wipe your feet and go into the parlour.'

An intrigued Rachel Munt now opened one eye ever so slightly, so that she could see what was going on. The kitchen was dark but she could see clearly as Celestina entered the room, for she was carrying a candle in front of her. Rachel saw that Celestina had changed her dress. She had gone out, half an hour before, in a black dress, but now she was wearing one with colourful flowers embroidered upon it. Celestina walked over to where Rachel lay, checked that the girl was indeed asleep, pulled down the window blind and left the room again.

A minute or so later, Celestina entered the kitchen again. She still carried the candle but now there was a young girl with her. Through her half-open eyelid, Rachel could not be sure who the girl was, but she knew she had seen her before, just a couple of weeks before. Rachel could also see that as Celestina walked across the kitchen, the girl stayed at the doorway leading to the rest of the house.

'What are you stopping for? Come in. What are you afraid of?' said Celestina, in a very quiet voice, no doubt concerned that she might wake Rachel. The girl replied: 'I am not afraid mamma, but it is a strange place to me. I have not been in this room before.' At that, Celestina crossed back to where the child stood, took her gently by the hand and led her to the cellar door. The couple then went into the cellar itself.

What happened next, filled Rachel Munt with terror. After a few minutes, she heard the girl call out: 'You are going to cut my throat?' To that Celestina coldly replied: 'I am going to kill you.' A now hysterical child's voice cried: 'You will go to the devil. The devil will have you.' This was followed by some awful sounds of scuffling and gurgling and, a few moments later, by a weak cry of: 'I am dying.'

Though Rachel could not see what horrors were taking place in that cellar, she could see the flickering light from the candle Celestina had taken with her. Now, as Rachel gazed at the doorway, the light was snapped off. Celestina had obviously blown the candle out for now she returned to the kitchen, closing the cellar door gently behind her.

Still the terrible act was not over, for now Celestina paced around the kitchen, occasionally going back down into the cellar and speaking to the child who she had taken into that room. At one stage Rachel heard her say: 'You bastard, I will kill you.' A few minutes later, Celestina said: 'I will teach you to tell any more lies about me.'

Throughout this period, Rachel could hear the child groaning from somewhere in the cellar. Finally, she saw Celestina re-light the candle, go back into the cellar and, after a slight pause, heard her say: 'There you bastard, you must be dead by this time.' She then returned to the kitchen and walked over to where Rachel lay.

Rachel Munt's heart beat wildly in her chest as her mistress tapped her twice on the shoulder and called her name. Fearful of what might happen to her if she revealed the slightest clue as to what she had just seen and heard, Rachel pretended that she had just been roused from her sleep and smiled broadly at Celestina, who then asked her to fetch some soap, as she wished to wash her hands before going to bed. Rachel did as Celestina asked and was relieved to see her then retire for the night.

Early the following morning, Sunday 17 February, Rachel Munt took a few tentative steps down into the cellar. There she found the body of the girl from the previous night, her face and hands covered in blood. It was clear that the poor girl was dead.

At 11.00am that same morning, Rachel's sister called to visit her. Rachel told her what had happened the night before, and even showed her sister the body of the girl in the cellar. It was Rachel's sister who ran to the nearest police station and told the officer on duty what had taken place at Linton Street.

It was Sergeant Edwin Townsend who visited the house later that same day. The door was opened by Celestina herself, who demanded to know what the officer wanted. Sergeant Townsend replied: 'To search your cellar.' To this, Celestina laughed and shouted: 'Look into my cellar. Good God, whatever for?'

At that point, Karl Somner came into the hallway from the parlour and, after Sergeant Townsend had identified himself to Karl, all three then went down into the cellar. There they found the body of the girl, lying on her back, her face partially turned to the right. There was a large gaping wound in her neck and a large amount of blood on the body and pooled around it.

'I did not do it' cried Celestina to her husband. She then continued: 'I did not tell you, as I did not wish to make you timid, but I heard a noise outside of the railings last night.'

Sergeant Townsend now made a search of the house. In the bedroom that Karl and Celestina shared he found the flowered gown, stained with blood. To explain this, Celestina said that she had recently suffered from a nose bleed. Townsend was having none of it. Celestina Somner was arrested and charged with murder.

Celestina made her appearance at the police court the following day, Monday, 18 February. Here she admitted that the dead child was ten-year-old Celestina Christmas and said that she was her brother's child. He had now gone away and left the child in Celestina's care. She, in turn, had placed the young girl with a Mrs Harrington who lived at 4 Peter Street, Hackney but, on 6 February, had taken the child away and left her with Mrs Groves, her married sister, who lived at 16 Murray Street. She could not explain how the child had come to be found dead in her cellar.

Sent for trial, Celestina Somner was originally due to appear before Mr Justice Wightman on 8 March, but the defence were not yet ready and the case was put back to April.

The main prosecution witness was, of course, Rachel Munt. After she had told her story, the prosecution called various witnesses, who were able to show that the dead girl had, in fact, been Celestina's own daughter. Celestina had been paying ten shillings per week for the girl's upkeep and it seemed likely that the motive for the crime was simply that she objected to paying out that cash for a daughter for whom she had no affection. It was also shown that the child, Celestina Christmas, was Celestina Somner's maiden name, the same name she had given to her illegitimate daughter.

Mrs Groves, the prisoner's sister, confirmed that the dead girl had lived with her for a short time. On the night that Celestina took her away, she told Mrs Groves that she had found a position for her daughter at a greengrocer's establishment, where she could earn her keep.

The final witness was Dr George W H Coward, the Divisional Police Surgeon. He had examined the body of the child and reported three large wounds in the throat, running from the back to the front and embracing the whole of the left side of the neck. The jugular vein had been divided on that side, and the carotid artery had been badly injured, though not cut through completely. The child also bore defence wounds on her left hand and arm.

With all the evidence against Celestina, the jury quickly returned their guilty verdict and the prisoner was duly sentenced to death. Twenty-six-year-old Celestina Somner did not, however, hang. In due course, perhaps somewhat surprisingly, her sentence was commuted to one of life imprisonment.

# Chapter 8

# Robert Robinson Tripp
## 1857

Edward Silence was in a deep sleep in the small hours of 7 April 1857, when a noise disturbed him. At first, Silence was unable to place the noise but, as he sat up in bed, he heard a voice calling him from the rooms upstairs.

Silence lodged in rooms, at 28 Gifford Street, and he knew that there was one other lodger in the house, Robert Tripp, an old man of sixty-two, who had the rooms upstairs. The voice Silence had heard, though, did not seem to be Tripp's. Rather it sounded like their landlord, thirty-three-year-old James Scott, a master baker, from Freeling Street, who also dabbled a little in property, and owned the house that Silence and Tripp lived in.

Going upstairs, Silence found both Tripp and Scott on the landing outside Tripp's room. It was very dark, but Silence could see that Mr Scott had some kind of paper in his hand. Scott then asked Silence if he would return to his own rooms, and bring up a light, so that they might see better. Silence did as his landlord asked, and was back, with a candle, a few minutes later.

As James Scott began to read from the paper, Silence knew that it was an official notice, informing Tripp that, because he was behind with his rent, his goods would be seized in order to cover the arrears. Tripp, meanwhile, had taken a key from his pocket, and now opened the door to his rooms. He paused briefly, and then dashed inside, for a moment or two, Tripp then returned to the landing with a large cutlass in his hand. Without another word, Tripp then plunged the blade into Scott's left side. As Scott staggered backwards, Tripp attempted to strike for a second time but Silence threw out his arm, and managed to push the weapon aside. Satisfied with what he had done, Robert Tripp walked into his rooms and calmly closed the door behind him.

It was obvious that Scott was very badly hurt. Edward Silence managed to get him downstairs, and supported him as they walked to the surgery of Dr Horatio Siliphant. It was 3.00am, by the time the doctor attended to Scott, but the wound was so severe, that he ordered Scott to be taken to his own home at Freeling Street, the doctor going with him, so that he could be treated in his own bed.

The police were informed of the attack and, as a result, Constable Benjamin Hill, who was on duty nearby, was despatched to Gifford Street to arrest Tripp. Hill arrived at Tripp's lodgings, and knocked boldly on the door. A voice from within asked who it was. Informed that it was the police, Tripp pointed out that the door was unlocked. and that they should come straight in.

Tripp was sitting in an easy chair, smoking his pipe. By the side of the chair, now safely in its scabbard, was a cutlass. Constable Hill informed Tripp that he wished to speak to him about the attack upon Mr Scott. Tripp replied: 'He is my landlord. I told him that I owed him some rent; that it was an unreasonable hour; and that if he would call on Saturday, I would pay. I persuaded him to go out, but he refused, and then I stabbed him.'

Hill asked Tripp what weapon he had used. Tripp nodded towards the weapon at the side of the chair and said: 'The cutlass, and I hope I have given him his death wound. If it had not been for Mr Silence, I would have cut his head off.'

On the way to the police station, Tripp asked Hill if Scott were dead. Told that he was not, but that his injury was severe, Tripp commented: 'I am sorry for that. I am sorry I have not given him his death wound.'

At the station, Tripp was seen by Sergeant George Beckley. Constable Hill informed his sergeant of the charge, and said that the injured man had been taken to the hospital. This was not the case, though Hill did not know that. Tripp merely said: 'If it had not been for the lodger, there would have been no occasion to take him to the hospital.'

Despite the ministrations of Dr Siliphant, James Scott died

from his wound at 1.30am on 8 April. The charge against Robert Tripp was then amended to one of wilful murder.

Tripp's trial took place at the Old Bailey, before Baron Watson, on 15 June 1857. The case for the prosecution was led by Mr Bodkin, who was assisted by Mr Robinson. Tripp was defended by Mr Metcalfe and Mr Orridge.

The first witness was Edward Silence, the man who lodged at the same address as the prisoner. Silence began by describing himself as a house painter, and confirmed that he occupied the ground floor at 28 Gifford Street, whilst Tripp occupied the first floor. At about 2.30am on 7 April, Silence had been woken by a noise. He got up and unlocked his door, whereupon he heard Mr Scott say: 'Mr. Silence, come up stairs.' Upon going up, Mr Scott had said: 'Mr Silence, can you get a light?' Almost as soon as he had done so, Tripp had gone into his room, returned holding the sword, and stabbed Mr. Scott. When he was struck, Scott staggered back against the hand rail and cried out: 'I am stabbed.'

After Constable Hill and Sergeant Beckley had given their evidence, the prosecution called George Willis. He was a house agent, and said he had called on the prisoner on 3 April. Whilst there, they had some conversation about an earlier occasion when Tripp had fallen into arrears with his rent.

That had been the previous November, and at that time, Scott had sent the bailiffs in and seized some of Tripp's belongings. They had then been sold off to pay the debt. Apparently this still upset Tripp, who said that he would not permit such a thing to ever happen again. Willis had suggested that if he was not happy living in Scott's house, he might be better off finding a new address. Tripp had replied that he would leave only when he wished to, and he would let no man put him out of his home.

Dr Siliphant, in addition to treating Scott's wound, had also performed the post-mortem after he had died. He reported a single deep wound on the left side. The blade of the cutlass used, had penetrated the intestines and cut through part of the bowel. That single wound was undoubtedly the direct cause of death.

In his summing up for the defence, Mr Metcalfe claimed that

his client had been sorely provoked. There could be no doubt that Tripp owed money to Mr Scott but the latter had actually behaved illegally. He was, of course, entitled to collect his rent but not at 2.30am in the morning. At the same time, whilst Tripp was an elderly man, Scott was a muscular, fit and well-built man. There was no suggestion that he had used any violence upon Tripp, but if he had done so, then the court would not be hearing a case of murder, as any man had the right to defend himself. The crime would, quite rightly, be reduced to one of manslaughter, and surely that should be the case now.

The jury retired to consider their verdict and, apparently, took the words of Mr Metcalfe to heart. They found Robert Tripp not guilty of murder, but guilty of manslaughter.

Before passing sentence, the trial judge pointed out that it was quite right that a man may defend himself, he must not use a weapon such as a cutlass, unless he were in fear of his life. That had not been the case in the killing of James Scott and, consequently, he saw no reason to award a lenient sentence. Tripp was then sentenced to eight years in prison.

# Chapter 9

# Thomas Robert Davis
## 1857

T hough it was completely erroneous, Thomas Davis had managed to convince himself that his wife, Mary Ann, had been having an affair with a soldier. It did not matter that he had no proof, or that he couldn't even name the soldier supposedly concerned in this liaison. The suspicion was there, and it preyed upon his mind.

On Tuesday 6 October 1857, Thomas and Mary Ann had been away from their home at 11 Dorset Street, Islington, for most of the day. At approximately 10.40pm, or perhaps a little later, they entered the *Royal George* public house, in Lower Road, where Thomas ordered a rum, and a pot of beer. He and Mary Ann, together with their four year old daughter, then sat quietly in a corner, where Thomas drank the rum, giving a sip to Mary Ann. In all, they were only in the pub for around three minutes before they left; Mary Ann carrying the child in her arms, and Thomas carrying the pot of beer.

They were seen in the street outside by two people, who knew them well. Mark Welch was a waiter at a different public house, the Royal William on Ball's Pond Road. He had just left work, and was walking down Lower Road, when he saw Thomas and Mary Ann walking down the street, heading in the direction of their home. Welch noticed that Thomas was very unsteady on his feet, and obviously the worse for drink.

The second person to see them close to the *Royal George*, was Edmund Phillips. He was a neighbour of the Davis's, living just around the corner from them, in Albion Road. He also thought that Thomas looked to be under the influence of drink, though he believed that Mary Ann was perfectly sober. He heard no cross words pass between them, as they passed him, and bade him goodnight.

Sarah Stromp and her husband, John, also lived in 11 Dorset Street. They had lodgings on the second floor, whilst Thomas and Mary Ann lived below them, on the first. By 11.30pm, both Sarah and John were in bed. Sarah was still awake, but John was asleep and snoring loudly.

The walls in the house were rather thin, and raised voices would always be heard, by the others who lived in the house. So, when an argument broke out between Thomas and Mary Ann, Sarah could hear clearly all that was said. Thomas began by accusing his wife of being a bloody soldier's whore, to which Mary Ann replied: 'No, Davis, I have enough with you. One is quite enough for me.' At that, Thomas said that he would get his razor, and settle this matter once and for all.

Fearful that something terrible was about to happen, Sarah Stromp woke her husband, and asked him to go downstairs, to speak to Thomas. Even as John was pulling on his trousers, a loud scream rang through the building, and Mary Ann cried: 'Murder!' three times.

John Stromp hurried downstairs, closely followed by his wife. They found Thomas standing near his bedroom door, a half open razor in his hand, dripping with blood. Mary Ann was staggering down the hallway, heading towards the front door, with her daughter clutched in her arms. She was bleeding profusely, from a vicious wound in her throat. So bad was the wound, that even her daughter was covered in the fast flowing crimson liquid.

As John Stromp held on to Thomas Davis, his wife, Sarah, ran out into the street, after Mary Ann who, by now, had placed her daughter on the ground. As Mary Ann ran into the middle of the street, her tearful and terrified daughter hung onto her nightdress, crying out for someone to help her mother.

The police were on the scene in minutes, alerted by the screams. By the time they had arrived, however, Mary Ann had breathed her last. Thomas Davis found himself arrested, taken to the Kingsland police station, and charged with the murder of his wife.

The trial took place at the Old Bailey just twenty days later, on 26 October. After Sarah Stromp had told her story, her husband stepped into the witness box. John Stromp testified that, upon seizing hold of the prisoner, he had asked: 'For God's sake, what have you done Davis?' Thomas had replied: 'Now I have done it, I am a happy man.' Seconds later he handed over the razor saying: 'This is what I have done it with.' He then asked John to let him go, so that he could go out into the yard at the back of the house. John refused to release him, saying that he would only let go when a constable had arrived to take him into custody.

Sarah Ann Day was another lodger at 11 Dorset Street, and she had also heard the loud argument between Thomas and his wife. She had also heard him call her a 'bloody soldier's whore'. Throughout the argument, and the subsequent attack upon Mary Ann, her daughter was begging for her parents to stop shouting at each other.

Mary Anne Harman also lived in Dorset Street, but at number 17. On the night in question, she had been out for a drink, and upon returning home, had opened her front window to let some air into the house, it being quite a warm night. She had heard the argument and the cries of 'Murder!' and, looking out of her window, saw Mary Ann Davis run into the street, blood pouring from a wound in her throat. By the time Mrs Harman had run out into the street to help her neighbour, she had collapsed into the arms of a gentleman passing by. Even as Mrs Harman took Mary Ann Davis into her own arms, she breathed her last and died.

Dr James Williamson had been called to the scene, by the police. By the time he arrived, Mary Ann was already dead. Dr Williamson made a careful examination, and saw a single wound, extending from the right side of the neck, across to the large muscles on the left. The jugular vein, on both sides of the neck, had been severed and the wind-pipe cut through. Mary Ann had lost a vast amount of blood, causing her death within minutes of the wound being inflicted.

Constable James Haliday was the first officer on the scene. He had been on patrol nearby, when he heard the cries for help. It was Haliday who arrested Thomas Davis.

Sergeant Henry Bovis had also been close to Dorset Street, and heard the cries. Going to Dorset Street, Bovis went up to Davis's rooms, and when Thomas saw him, he merely said: 'Well, sergeant, shake hands with me.'

Thomas was escorted to the Kingsland police station, where he arrived at 12.50am on Wednesday 7 October. He was seen by Inspector George Langdon, who felt that the prisoner was too drunk to be interviewed at that stage. Later, at around 3.00am, Thomas asked to see the Inspector, to whom he made a brief statement, admitting responsibility for the crime.

That confession, together with the testimony of the various witnesses, meant that the guilty verdict was little more than a formality. Sentenced to death, Thomas Robert Davis was hanged outside Newgate prison on Monday 16 November 1857. Justice had certainly moved very quickly. It was a day short of six weeks, since Thomas had taken Mary Ann's life.

# Chapter 10

# Sarah Sadler
# 1861

William John Brooks Collins ran a baker's shop, from premises at 8 Scott's Place, Lower Road, Islington. He lived there with Sarah Sadler, his common-law wife, and his daughter from a previous relationship, Jane Collins. Whilst William was a social drinker, only taking the occasional glass, Sarah liked to imbibe freely and, once she was in drink, would become very argumentative.

On Tuesday 11 December 1860 Sarah was, once again, proving to be rather difficult, and yet another argument ensued. To keep the peace, William suggested that they should go for a drink, at the nearby *Crown* public house. Sarah agreed, but the visit to the Crown did nothing to soothe her temper. She carried on arguing, and things became so bad, that William asked the landlord to put Sarah out into the street. The landlord was more than happy to oblige, and Sarah was thrown out, leaving William to finish his pint in peace.

It was around 9.00pm when William left the *Crown*, only to find Sarah waiting outside for him. She greeted him with foul language, and then lashed out at him, knocking his hat from his head. A weary William bent down, picked up his hat, and without saying a word to Sarah, walked back towards the bakery. Sarah followed and, at the moment William walked through his doorway, she formed a double fist and struck William violently on the right side of his head. Sarah then ran off into the street, and did not return to Scott's Place again.

This attack was witnessed by Jane Collins, who was behind the counter, inside the shop. She saw her father stagger forward and, had it not been for the fact that he slumped into a chair, William would certainly have fallen to the floor. Jane went to minister to her father, who said his head was hurting from the blow, and that he had better go up to bed.

The next morning, 12 December, William rose at his usual early hour and began operating his business. His head, though, was still very painful and he found that after just a couple of hours work, he needed to retire back to his bed. Jane took care of her father for the rest of the day.

Over the next few days, this was repeated. William would try to maintain his usual routine, but each day he found that he could not work more than a couple of hours. Most of the time he was back in bed, hoping that the pain in his head would eventually pass.

By Monday 17 December, things had grown so bad that Jane felt that she had no choice but to call in the doctor. Dr Charles Seymour Thane duly attended, and found his patient suffering from an acute pain in his head, a violent cough, shivering and vomiting. Over the next few days, Dr Thane continued to administer medical treatment, but William Collins did not improve.

On Thursday 20 December, Sarah Sadler called on Dr Thane at his surgery, and asked how William Collins was. The doctor informed her that he believed that his patient was close to death, and that the authorities had been informed of her attack upon William, and were now looking for her.

Three days later, on 23 December, Sarah was arrested by Constable Herbert Stammers. He informed her that she was being taken for striking William Collins, and placing his life in danger. Sarah replied: 'Me strike him? I never struck him.' Reminded that it was likely that William would die, Sarah retorted: 'He will never die. He has been dying this four years, but if he was here now, I would give him something, if I get hung for it.'

On 1 January 1861, William Collins died, and Sarah found herself facing a charge of manslaughter. She appeared in court to answer that charge on 28 January.

James Lovett was a friend of William Collins, and had heard many arguments between him and the prisoner. On 11

December, Lovett had been in the *Crown*, had witnessed the latest argument, and Sarah being put out into the street. As she was escorted out she shouted: 'This penny I have got in my hand, I'll bury in your head tonight.' Lovett had left the *Crown* at about the same time as William, and saw Sarah knock his hat off.

James Easey, a cheesemonger, lived next door but one to William, at 4 Scott's Place. He had been at the front door of his shop on 11 December, and saw Sarah knock William's hat off. He also saw her strike William with a double fist, as he entered his own shop.

Dr Thane informed the court that he had performed a post-mortem on William and had found no external marks of violence whatsoever. Upon opening the body, Dr Thane found an effusion of blood on the brain, and believed that the cause of death was an inflammation of the membrane of the brain, brought on by the blow he had received from Sarah. However, when questioned by Sarah, Dr Thane also had to admit that he had treated William some three months before when he had been attacked and robbed by a group of men in Green Man's Lane. William had been knocked about, and was very bruised, but Dr Thane said he did not believe that an attack three months before could have contributed to William's death. Further questioning, however, brought the admission that both of William's lungs were very diseased, though he could well have lived for a few more years.

It was, perhaps, those doubts over the medical evidence, which caused the jury, after a short deliberation, to file back into court and announce that they had found Sarah Sadler not guilty of manslaughter. She then walked free from court, possibly a very fortunate woman indeed.

# Chapter 11

# William Henry Clarke
# 1863

On the evening of Sunday 30 March 1862, at around 8.00pm, Susan Hunter took her three children to a prayer meting, close to their home. The meeting finished some time before 10.00pm, and as Susan walked home with her three daughters, the eldest, Charlotte, asked if they might have some sweets. Susan reached into her purse and brought out a half-penny. She then returned home, leaving her children at the bottom of Greenman's Lane.

Charlotte Hunter took her two sisters, the youngest of whom she carried in her arms, to a sweetshop, where she purchased some sugar sticks. The children then crossed back over the road, and sat down on a doorstep to enjoy their treat. It was then that a man approached them.

The man spoke to Charlotte's younger sister, Elizabeth Anne Hunter, who was seven years and eight months old. He asked her if she would post a letter for him, to an address in William Street, and said he would give her two pence if she agreed. It was Charlotte who replied on her sister's behalf, saying that she must not go with the man. The man ignored this, took Elizabeth by the hand, and walked off down the street with her.

Charlotte was most distressed with this and, scooping her youngest sister into her arms again, set off to follow the man who had taken Elizabeth away. Curiously, he walked towards William Street, and Charlotte could not help but wonder why the man had not posted his own letter, if he was actually heading in that direction. Then, as Charlotte reached the end of William Street itself, a sudden gust of wind took her hat off. By the time she had managed to retrieve it, the man, and Elizabeth, had vanished.

A most tearful Charlotte returned home, and told her mother and father what had happened. They went out to look for Elizabeth and, when they could not find her, reported her missing to the police. A search was made, but no trace of either Elizabeth, or the man who had taken her, could be found. The reports in the newspapers grew fewer and fewer, and the police investigation was scaled down. Elizabeth Hunter had, seemingly, vanished from the face of the earth.

Time passed, and it was not until over a year later, on 6 July 1863, that a rather nervous Charles Martin walked into the police station, and told a very strange story indeed.

Martin explained that he had heard two men, William Cope and William Westmacott, having a curious conversation together. Something about a skull was mentioned so later, when Cope was alone, Martin asked him what he had been discussing. It was then that Cope informed Martin that they had been talking about an event that had taken place at work, some eight or nine months previously.

Cope, Westmacott and Martin had all worked at a nursery, on New North Road, as had another man, a youth named Samuel Strafford. One day, Strafford had been raking over a bed of soil, when he had unearthed a human skull. Strafford had taken this information to the owner of the nursery, one George Rowe. Rowe's reaction had been strange, to say the least. He had ordered Strafford to rebury the skull and say nothing about it.

Having listened to this story, Inspector Wisemen ordered two constables to go to the nursery, and make an examination of the flowerbed themselves. Some bones were indeed found but, when these were subject to analysis, they were found to belong to a dog. Strafford, however, persisted in his story so the search was renewed. On the second visit, a more careful search of the bed was made and an almost complete human skeleton was recovered. The bones, it was clear, belonged to a female child, aged about eight years old.

It was impossible to positively identify the skeleton but, it seemed reasonable to assume that the bones belonged to Elizabeth Anne Hunter. She was the right age, and she had been the only child to have disappeared in the immediate area. The problem now, was who was responsible for her death?

In fact, the name of a possible suspect, was immediately passed on to the police. George Rowe, who was not, rather curiously, questioned in depth about why he might have wished to conceal a human skull found on his premises, told the police that at the time Elizabeth had been abducted, he had employed a young man named William Henry Clarke. Further, Rowe knew for a fact, that seventeen-year-old Clarke, had a predilection for young girls, and had already assaulted two by the time Elizabeth vanished. As a result of that information, Clarke was arrested on 7 July 1863, the day after the skeleton had been found.

In effect, Clarke was tried for murder by the coroner. The inquest, which met three times at the *Florence Tavern*, on Florence Street, off Upper Street, had to determine if the skeleton was that of Elizabeth Hunter, if she had been murdered, and if there was enough evidence against Clarke to send him for trial.

Charlotte Hunter told the court of her sister's disappearance on 30 March, the previous year. That night had been a particularly wet, windy and misty one, and it had been deduced that visibility was around fifty yards, at best. When Charlotte described, using a map produced by the court, where she had been, and where her sister and the man had been, at the time she had last seen her, the distance was shown to be eighty-four yards. Of more import, however, was the fact that Charlotte did not think that the man who led Elizabeth away, was the man in the court: William Clarke.

The behaviour, in court, of George Rowe, was most unusual. Asked to give some personal details about himself, Rowe would only admit that he did not use his real name, and had not done so for a number of years. He refused to give his real name, or to say anything about his past. He was not pressed on what, if anything, he might be trying to hide. He was questioned only about Clarke.

Rowe confirmed that at the time of Elizabeth's disappearance, he had lodged at 5 Oxford Street, Islington. Clarke, who he employed, had also lodged at the house, the landlady being Charlotte Jennings. Clarke held the keys to the nursery, and it was his job to be there first each morning, and light the fires in the offices and greenhouses.

Rowe seemed to have a particular memory of the night of 30 March, the night Elizabeth Hunter was taken. Rowe claimed that this was because he had suffered a rather bad illness in mid-March, and was only just recovering at the end of the month. He recalled one night in particular, which he was certain was 30 March itself. On that night, he had told his landlady that if Clarke had not returned home by 10.00pm, then he must be refused admittance for the night. Clarke had indeed returned late, closer to 11.00pm, and, at Rowe's instructions, Mrs Jennings had refused to let him in. The following morning, Clarke had told Rowe, and his workmates, that he had gone back to the nursery and slept in the greenhouse. It was the same place that the skeleton had been found.

In the final part of his evidence, Rowe said that he knew of two previous occasions, where Clarke had assaulted young girls. In one of the cases, the mother of the child had made a complaint to him, and Rowe had spoken to Clarke about it. He had told Clarke that if he did not admit what he had done, then the mother would make a formal complaint to the police and Clarke would be arrested and charged. If, however, he signed a confession, then she would not proceed with the matter. Clarke had, rather reluctantly, admitted the offence and signed a paper to that effect.

Asked if he had any questions of this witness, Clarke began by trying to probe some of George Rowe's secrets. Clarke demanded to know if his real name were George Nicholls Simmons but Rowe refused to answer. Clarke then asked if it were true that he had once been the town clerk at Truro. Again, Rowe refused to answer and at that point, the coroner ordered that this line of questioning was not relevant to the present inquiry.

Charles Martin told the court about the conversation he had

overheard between Westmacott and Cope. He also said, that he had been informed that the reason Mr Rowe had given for not reporting the matter to the police, was that he felt that it might give the nursery a bad name.

William Cope testified that he had been talking to Westmacott, about the finding of a skull, by a boy named Strafford. He had not known that the flowerbed held a full human skeleton. The man he had been talking to, William Westmacott, confirmed the conversation, and said he had been present when Mr Rowe ordered it to be reburied.

Charlotte Jennings did testify that there had been a night, towards the end of March 1862, when Clarke had been refused admission to his lodgings, on Rowe's instructions. She was, however, unable to confirm that it had been the 30th. She too had been told, the following morning, that Clarke said he had slept in the greenhouse. She did not explain why Mr Rowe, who was only another lodger, should be giving her instructions as to who she should allow in the house, and who she should turn away.

An important witness would have been Samuel Strafford, the young man who had raked up the skull in the first place. Since that time, however, he had left the nursery, and had gone to live in Canada. He was somewhere in the wilderness, and even his own family had no idea where he was. The court was unable to contact him.

Further bad luck came with the evidence of sixteen-year-old Thomas Shrosbee. At the time Elizabeth had been taken, she had been wearing a rather distinctive pair of golden earrings. One of the pair was a good deal wider than the other, and these earrings had not been found with the skeleton. When details of those earrings were published in the newspapers, Thomas's father, William Shrosbee, had come forward to speak to the police.

William explained that his son had a pair of earrings, which fitted the description of the missing pair. Thomas worked in Church Street, Shoreditch, and in April 1863, he had come home with the earrings, which he had purchased from a man, for 3d. Those earrings were now produced in court, and although Susan Hunter, the missing girl's mother, could not be one hundred per cent sure that they were Elizabeth's, she did describe them as almost identical.

Shortly before the skeleton had been found, Thomas had fallen ill and been taken to St Bartholomew's Hospital. He had been interviewed there and said, to the police, that he would be able to make a positive identification of the man who sold the earrings to him. Unfortunately, since that time, Thomas's condition had worsened and he had since died. Whilst it was true that the description he had given, matched Clarke, it was so vague that it also matched another dozen men in the courtroom.

Another promising lead came from William Taylor. He had come forward at the time Elizabeth had been taken, and was now called to give his evidence in court. He said that he had been close to the nursery at around 10.00pm on 30 March 1862, when he had seen a young man, with a young girl. As Taylor passed them on the opposite side of the street, the man scooped the little girl up into his arms and walked on, towards the nursery. Taylor too, believed that he could positively identify the man he had seen. Asked to look around the court to see if the man was there, Taylor failed to pick out Clarke, or indeed anyone else.

William Clarke was now asked to take the stand and give his own account of things. Turning to the night of 30 March 1862, Clarke agreed that this had been the night that he had been locked out of his lodgings. He then called two witnesses, to prove that he had not slept in the greenhouse where the skeleton was later discovered.

The first of those witnesses was Clarke's mother, Sophia. She now lived in Lever Street, but at the time, had lived at 4 Ashby Street. She told the court, that her son had arrived at her house on the last Sunday in March, complaining that his landlady would not let him into his lodgings. He stayed with her that night.

It might be expected, that a mother would, perhaps, lie to protect her son, but the second witness, Maria Lee, was nothing more than a family acquaintance. She had called at Mrs Clarke's early on the evening of 30 March, and the door had been opened by William. Maria had stayed for some hours, and William was at home all that time.

In a further effort to convince the jury that Clarke was some kind of sexual pervert, the two girls he was supposed to have assaulted, were then called to give their evidence. The first of these, Mary Ann Baxter, said that she was now thirteen, but had been twelve at the time Clarke had attacked her. He had offered her some money to take a letter to William Street but instead had taken her into the greenhouse at the nursery. There he had touched her lower legs and placed a handkerchief over her face but, when she screamed, he let her go. It was Mary's mother who later had made a complaint to Mr Rowe.

The second girl, Mary Ann Lambert, said that Clarke had gone a little further. He had placed his hand up her clothing, onto her thigh. She had not made a complaint to the police, but had told her mother what had happened.

Having heard all the evidence, the jury decided that there was not sufficient evidence to send Clarke for trial on a charge of murder. They returned a verdict that the skeleton was that of Elizabeth Hunter, and that she had been murdered by a person or persons unknown. It was not, however, the end of Clarke's ordeal. He was remanded in custody on a charge of sexually assaulting the two young girls.

By the time he appeared at the Old Bailey to answer those charges, on 17 August, a third charge had been added. Now it was claimed that he had also sexually assaulted a girl named Sophia Allen. Despite his denials, the jury found him guilty of assaulting Mary Ann Baxter and Mary Ann Lambert, but not guilty of the assault upon Sophia Allen. For those two offences, Clarke was jailed for two years.

Was Clarke responsible for the death of Elizabeth Hunter? It seemed clear that the killer, whoever he was, seemed to have a modus operandi which involved young girls posting a letter for him, in William Street, and the two girls who said that Clarke sexually assaulted them, both said that he had used that phrase to entice them. However, one must not forget the strange behaviour of George Rowe who did not wish his past to be exposed, and who had simply hidden the discovery of a human skull on his property.

Research shows that George Rowe was, almost certainly, the man Clarke named: George Nicholls Simmons. George Simmons had been elected town clerk of Truro on 20 October 1837, when he was twenty-six-years-old, and eventually resigned in November 1859. His age, at that time, showed that he was born in 1811.

In August 1854, Simmonds, who was also a qualfied solicitor, acted as the corporation's representative in a dispute with a Mr Baynard, over who owned the soil in the river at Truro. When Simmonds finally submitted his bill, the legal costs came to £1,176, a considerable sum (worth over £50,000 today), and the council argued that they should not have to pay such a sum, and asked him to explain the figure. The matter rumbled on for a number of years with claim and counter claim being made. This led to animosity between Simmonds, and certain councillors, and may well have led to his resignation five years later, and his leaving of Cornwall, for London.

Further research shows that George Nicholls Simmonds, the only example of such a name, died in Islington, in the early part of 1874, when he was aged sixty-four, which would agree with a date of birth in either 1810 or 1811. That is too much for coincidence, and seems to indicate that Rowe and Simmonds were one and the same. It does not, however, explain why he should be so worried about hiding his past, unless there were those, in Truro, who were still looking for monies to be repaid.

# Chapter 12

# Charles Frederick Bricknell
# 1864

Wednesday 8 June 1864 had been a busy night at the *Lion Tavern* in North Road, at the New Metropolitan Cattle Market. Now, at around 11.15pm, the last customers were drinking up, and some of the staff were cleaning the various rooms.

Henry Keeble, the nephew of the landlord, was in the bar when a loud, long, blood-curdling scream rang out. The pitiful sound had come from upstairs, and Henry ran off to see what the problem was. He had only gone up a few of the stairs when he met Charles Frederick Bricknell coming down, a bloody knife in his hand. Bricknell looked at Keeble, and in a soft, gentle voice said: 'I ve done it Mr Henry. I have killed her. Take the knife.' As Keeble took the weapon from Bricknell, and seized him in case he should try to escape, he could not help but see, on the landing at the top if the stairs, the body of Jane Geary, one of the housemaids. Keeble then escorted Bricknell down to the bar, where he handed him over to a customer whilst he ran off to fetch the doctor and a policeman.

It was 11.30pm when Constable George Govers arrived at the *Lion Tavern*. By now, Bricknell was at the front of the bar, being guarded by other members of staff. He was handed over to Govers, and told that he would be arrested. He immediately volunteered: 'I will tell you all about it.' Constable Govers, quite correctly, cautioned his prisoner, that anything he said would be taken down and might be used in evidence. After listening carefully to the caution, Bricknell merely commented: 'She is the only girl I ever loved; and poor girl, she has got it, and I hope she will die.'

Dr George Tate was already in attendance, and at that moment he came down the stairs to announce that Jane Geary was dead.

Upon hearing this, Bricknell remarked: 'I would rather she were dead than anyone else should have her.' He was then escorted to the police station, where he was charged with murder.

Bricknell appeared at the Old Bailey on 11 July 1864. The case for the Crown was led by Mr Giffard, who was assisted by Mr Rowden. Bricknell's defence was detailed by Mr Sleigh, who wished to argue that this was a case of manslaughter, not murder.

Initially, details of the relationship of both the accused and his victim were given. Both had worked at the *Lion Tavern* for approximately two years and had, apparently, grown fond of each other. They had been walking out together for a few months but, the relationship had, apparently, cooled over the last few weeks. One day, a couple of weeks before Jane was killed, one of her cousins had visited her, at the public house. He had been a most affable fellow, and had enjoyed a pint with two of the male members of staff before he left. Ever since that time, Jane had behaved towards Bricknell in a much more offhanded manner, and he had managed to persuade himself that Jane was involved with her cousin. Indeed, at the time the cousin was enjoying his drink in the bar, Bricknell had remarked to a fellow worker: 'That is the man that had taken my peace of mind.'

The first witness was Henry Keeble. He confirmed that Jane had been a housemaid, whilst Bricknell had been employed as an under-waiter. Keeble claimed that he had been unaware, that there had been any relationship between Jane and the accused and, as far as he was concerned, they had merely been workmates.

William Gardner was the head-waiter and, at the time of Jane's scream, he was in the front bar, sweeping the floor. He had followed Henry Keeble up the stairs and saw him seize Bricknell. Gardner had then pushed past them, and continued on up to the landing, where he found Jane bleeding profusely from a wound in her left breast. As he watched, she quivered a little, and tried to draw a breath, but then sank back. As Gardner cradled her in his arms, he knew that she was already dead.

In addition to attending to the victim at the scene, Dr Tate had also performed the post-mortem. He found a single incised wound on the upper part of her left breast, and measured it at almost two inches deep. The knife had passed through Jane's left lung, and on into the heart. Death must have been almost instantaneous, and considerable force would have been needed to inflict the fatal wound.

Thomas Charles Hill also worked at the *Tavern*. He stated that just a few minutes before the attack upon Jane, Bricknell had come into his bedroom. They had talked for a while, and then Charles had said good night. Bricknell had commented: 'Oh, I might come down again.' Minutes later he had stabbed Jane. It had been Hill, to whom Bricknell had made the remark, that Jane's cousin had taken his peace of mind.

Mary Platten, was another chambermaid at the *Tavern*, and she had shared a room with Jane Geary. A few weeks before, Jane had asked Mary's advice, about walking out with Bricknell, and Mary had offered the opinion that she did not think it a good idea. This was not because she disapproved of Bricknell, but simply because she did not think Jane should be associating with someone she worked with.

On the night of Jane's death, she and Mary had gone up to bed together. On the landing, Mary remembered that one of the guests, who was staying at the *Tavern*, had not come in yet. She had told Jane that she would have to go downstairs, quickly, and tell the other staff members to expect him later. Jane said she would wait for her on the landing. Less than a minute later, just as Mary was at the foot of the stairs, that terrible scream rang out as Jane was stabbed.

For the defence, Mr Sleigh tried to persuade the jury, that his client was so distressed, over the cooling of his relationship with the love of his life, that his mind was unbalanced at the time, and he should, therefore, only be found guilty of manslaughter. The jury did not agree with that argument and found Bricknell guilty of murder.

Sentenced to death, Charles Frederick Bricknell was executed, outside the Old Bailey, at 8.00am on Tuesday 1 August 1864, by William Calcraft. The newspapers of the day described the crowd as largely well behaved. However, a nine-year-old girl was accidentally knocked down and trodden on by the mob. She suffered a broken leg and other more minor injuries.

# Chapter 13

# Mary Eliza Rorke
## 1864

On Friday 11 July 1863, Maria Harding left her lodgings at 4 Lempster Terrace, James Street, Islington, to move to a new address. As a result, the landlord of the property, George Moring, visited the house a number of times, to prepare her rooms for a new tenant.

Moring's first visit took place at around 10.00am on Saturday 12 July. It was whilst he was at Lempster Terrace, that he noticed, in one of the other rooms, a child, some six months old, lying on a pile of rags on the floor, in an absolutely filthy condition.

The child was William Joseph Rorke, and of his mother, Mary Eliza, there was no sign. In all, Moring spent five or six hours at the house and it was not until late that afternoon that Mary Eliza returned, obviously the worse for drink. Rather surprisingly, Moring said nothing to her about leaving her young son alone for so many hours.

On Monday 14 July, Moring was back at the house at 9.00am. This time, Mary Eliza Rorke was there, and appeared to be sober, but her child was still in the same dirty condition. Yet again, Moring did nothing, beyond telling Mary Rorke that he might well want her to find fresh lodgings.

Another visit took place on the evening of Tuesday 15 July. Once again, the child was alone, and still in an apparently neglected condition, but Mary returned soon afterwards, again the worse for drink. George Moring had now made three visits to the house, and done nothing to report the state of the child to the authorities.

Ann Molloy had been another of Moring's tenants at 4 Lempster Terrace, but she had left the house on 10 July. On the afternoon of Wednesday 16 July, Ann returned to the house to collect some items she had left behind. She, for the first time, saw William Rorke alone on his bundle of filthy rags, and decided to do something about it. Ann wasted no time in finding a constable and told him that there was a neglected child, alone in Lempster Terrace.

Constable Frederick White found the boy lying in the right hand corner of a back room, on a pillow made from a number of rags tied together. Not only was the child in a deplorable condition, having not been washed for some time, but it was also clear that he was very ill indeed. Dr John Bubbers Mather was sent for and, after seeing that the child was given some warm milk to nourish it, Dr Mather ordered William to be removed to the Islington workhouse. Unfortunately, it had all come too late. Though he was bathed, changed and taken care of, William Joseph Rorke died at the workhouse, at 4.00pm that same day. A warrant was now issued for the arrest of Mary Eliza Rorke, on a charge of manslaughter.

In fact, Mary had seen a crowd of people around the house, as she had been returning to it. Convinced that the authorities were now looking for her, she turned on her heel, and vanished into the streets of Islington. Police officers on the beat were told to be on the look-out for her, but it was not until 29 February, of the following year, that she was finally found and taken into custody.

Mary Rorke appeared at the Old Bailey, to answer the charge of manslaughter, on 11 April 1864. In addition to the witnesses already mentioned, the prosecution called Dr John Robert Ede.

Dr Ede was the Medical Officer at the Islington workhouse. He testified that the child had been brought into his establishment at 1.30pm on 16 July of the previous year. The boy had been very emaciated and was suffering from diarrhoea. Despite being cleaned, and fed, William died a few hours later. Dr Ede had later performed the post-mortem and deduced that the cause of death was emaciation and neglect.

Dr Arthur Henry Sanson practised from a surgery in Angel Terrace, and he testified that on 7 July 1863, William Rorke had been brought to him, by his mother. The child was suffering from very bad diarrhoea and he prescribed some medicine for it. This medicine had been found in the house at 4 Lempster Terrace, and about half of it had been used.

There were, however, other witnesses, who seemed to show that Mary Rorke had not, in fact, neglected her son. Mary Ann Cooper was another lodger at Lempster Terrace, and she told the court that sometimes, she had helped Mary by taking care of William for her. The child was fed regularly and looked after, but he had been ill since birth. It was true that William was often left alone, and was in a dirty condition, but that was due to his illness. When she came home, Mary would feed and change the child but he did not seem to thrive, and within hours of being bathed, was again covered in filth.

This testimony was confirmed by Jesse Eliza Rorke, Mary's seventeen-year-old daughter. Though Jesse did not live with her mother, she did visit her regularly. She told the court that William had been weak from birth, and indeed, had not been expected to survive when he was first born. Mary had done all she could for the child, and Jesse was surprised that he had even lived for six months.

The verdict, when it came, was that Mary Eliza Rorke was not guilty of manslaughter and she walked from court a free woman. Perhaps the life of William Rorke might have been saved, had he received proper medical treatment weeks, or even days earlier. He might also have fared better had his mother's landlord bothered to report the matter when he first saw the child in such a deplorable condition.

# Chapter 14

# George Campbell
## 1868

On 25 December 1868, people all over London, and indeed the rest of the country, were celebrating Christmas. It was no different at 42 Alfred Street, in Islington, where a large number of people were enjoying each other's company.

The house was actually owned by the Wotherspoon family. Two of them, Alexander Ferguson Wotherspoon and his brother, Archibald, were present. Also there were two other brothers: John and James Moir and two friends of theirs, George Campbell and George Bell. Everyone was having a good time and, though alcohol was being consumed, nobody appeared to be the worse for its effects.

The night drew on, and at one stage, Campbell sat down near James Moir, seemingly very depressed indeed. James did not really need to ask Campbell what was worrying him, for he had been present at the event, which was causing him so much misery.

George Campbell and the Moir brothers all originally hailed from Largs, in Scotland, and all were now employed as upholsterers, in London. Some two weeks before Christmas, Campbell and James Moir had been out together and, after a night's drinking, had brought two women back to the house in Alfred Street. The two men had paired off with the women, and both had had sex with their respective partners. For James, this was nothing more than a night of unrestrained pleasure, but for Campbell it meant much more. He had a girlfriend back in Scotland, to whom he had now been unfaithful. The guilt had been eating away at him ever since, and it did not help that James appeared to have a clear conscience over the events of that night.

After sitting for a few minutes, Campbell rose and went out of the room. He was heading upstairs, when Alexander Wotherspoon saw him and asked him where he was going. Campbell replied: 'Will you come upstairs and have a quiet drop of rum?' Alexander agreed, and followed his friend up. Overhearing the comment, twenty-three-year-old John Moir, went with them.

Inside one of the bedrooms, John Moir said that they should have a sing song, and he went to find his copy of the Christy Minstrel's Song Book. When he returned, rather than have a song, Campbell said that he could wrestle Moir. A puzzled John Moir replied: 'We did not come here to wrestle.'

Not to be dissuaded, Campbell now offered to spar with Moir. John said, jokingly, that he could probably take Campbell with one hand, but added that they had not come there to fight either. At that, Campbell walked across to a cupboard, which had a rifle on the wall above it. He began to take the rifle down from its mounting and John Moir, growing ever concerned over his friend's erratic behaviour, tried to prevent him. There was a brief struggle, and the bayonet fell off the muzzle of the weapon. As John Moir bent down to pick the bayonet up, Campbell left the room, taking the rifle with him.

A few minutes later, Campbell returned, still carrying the rifle. He stood for a few moments, looking into the room from the doorway, until suddenly he shouldered the rifle and pointed it towards the window. John Moir asked him what he was going to do. Indicating an oil lamp with a nod of his head, Campbell replied: 'I am going to put that lamp out.'

The rifle was duly pointed towards the lamp, and it did not seem to bother Campbell that both Moir and Wotherspoon were in the direct line of fire. There was a flash and a loud report as Campbell pulled the trigger. Instantly, John Moir fell to the floor, the bullet striking him to the left side of his nose, just below his eye.

Alexander Wotherspoon called for his brother, Archibald, and told him to run for a doctor. It being Christmas night, of course, Archibald had great difficulty in finding one who would come out. He visited two medical gentlemen, both of whom were at home, but both of whom refused to attend. It was not until he called on the third doctor, that Archibald found one who would come to the house, and attend to the man who had been shot.

Dr Joseph Ricksby Donald confirmed that John Moir was dead, and saw that his brain was protruding from the wound. A cursory examination showed that the bullet had not penetrated his brain, but had fractured his skull and forced the broken bone into his head. Dr Donald was also able to confirm that no doctor would have been able to help, as Moir would have been dead before his body hit the floor. As for the bullet, it had apparently bounced off Moir's head, then hit a wall, and had finally come to rest on a sofa.

The first police officer to arrive at the house was Constable Jabez Jeanes who, going into the room, saw Moir lying on his left side in a large pool of blood. On the floor, close by the body, lay a rifle. Jeanes asked who had fired the fatal shot, whereupon the others in the house pointed out Campbell. Told that he would be charged with murder, Campbell replied: 'I did not do it.'

George Campbell's trial for murder took place on 11 January 1869. Archibald Wotherspoon told the court that he had seen his brother leave the front parlour at around 7.00pm, on Christmas Day. Some ten minutes later he heard a shot from upstairs and rushed up to investigate. Seeing John Moir lying on the floor, in a widening pool of blood, and Campbell sitting in a chair with the rifle propped up against it, Archibald said: 'George, have you done this?' Campbell, looking rather shocked, had replied: 'No, I have not done it. I have done nothing.' He then paused for a few seconds, before adding: 'I liked Jack, and I don't mind swinging for him.'

Some of Campbell's history was also detailed in court. Some years ago, Campbell had been in the Army, serving in the 5th Dragoons, but had bought himself out. Campbell had returned to Largs, and began working as an upholsterer. In September of 1867, James Moir had returned to Largs to visit some of his family. The two men had met up, and when James returned to London, Campbell had gone with him and shared his lodgings in Alfred Street. Indeed, all three men, the Moir brothers and Campbell, shared the same bedroom.

Perhaps one of the most telling parts of the evidence, was a comment Campbell had made after his arrest. Referring to the woman he had slept with, and the shooting of John Moir he was reported to have said: 'I did one foolish thing that night; I have now done a second; and I shall do a third, and then you will know about it.' If the jury came to believe that this particular phrase showed any degree of premeditation on Campbell's part, then he would be guilty of murder, and would face the hangman's noose.

The jury, however, came to believe that whilst Campbell had undoubtedly taken John Moir's life, it had been an accidental shooting. Consequently, they found him not guilty of murder, but guilty of manslaughter. For that offence he received the rather light sentence of one year in prison.

# Chapter 15

# Susan King
## 1871

On 2 March 1871, Annie Butcher gave birth to a baby girl, who she named Alice. Annie was an unmarried mother and, although she did get a regular allowance from the baby's father, she could not really afford to keep the child. As a result, she handed the baby over to a woman who already had five children of her own: Susan King.

Forty-four-year-old Susan King lived in Arundel Grove, Kingsland Road, Islington and, for taking care of Alice, received the sum of six shillings per week. When Alice was handed over she was a healthy, robust child, and her mother visited her once every week.

As time passed, Annie Butcher's visits became less frequent. So much so that by early September, she had not seen her daughter for some three weeks. Still, she had no cause for concern. After all, Susan had already brought up five children and there could be little doubt that Alice was in good hands. Annie, however, was mistaken, and those people, who lodged at the same house as Susan King, saw a different side of things.

Emma Mills was one of those fellow lodgers, and she saw little Alice on an almost daily basis. Susan was often out of the house, and left the baby in the care of her own children. They took no interest in Alice's welfare, and the child was often heard crying for hours on end. There was also the fact that whenever Emma did see the baby, she seemed to be dirty and dishevelled.

On Saturday 16 September, Emma Mills was home for most of the day. The sound of Alice crying loudly, seemed to go on for hours and hours until, finally, Emma had had enough. She went up to Susan's rooms, intent on giving her a piece of her mind for neglecting the baby, but Susan was not at home.

Some of Susan's own children were there, and Emma demanded to see the baby. Taken to view her in her cot, Emma saw that she was absolutely filthy. Alice was dressed only in a thin nightdress, and was wet, right up to her neck. It was time to take this matter to the authorities. That same day, Emma walked into her local police station and reported the neglect of the child.

It took two days for the report to filter through to the correct department, and on Monday 18 September, at 7.00pm, Edwin Leonard Merchan, one of the relieving officers for Islington, visited the house at Arundel Grove. He found Alice in a cradle in the corner of one of the rooms. She was, again, absolutely filthy, and had obviously not been changed for some time. There was excrement right up to the lower part of the baby's neck. Mr Merchan then left the premises, to report the matter to Dr Duckett.

At 10.00pm, Merchan and Dr Andrew David Duckett, returned to Arundel Grove. By now, Alice had been washed and changed, her children having informed Susan King of Mr Merchan's earlier visit, but an examination showed that Alice was badly malnourished. She also had a number of sores on her body, almost certainly caused by irritation from lying in urine and faeces on a regular basis. Dr Duckett ordered that the child be removed to a safer house. That same night, little Alice Butcher was handed over to Mrs Jane Wells.

When Jane Wells received Alice, the very first thing she did, was weigh her. Alice, by now six months old, weighed just five and a half pounds. Now, for the first time, since she had been handed over to Susan King, Alice was given proper care and feeding. Unfortunately, it had all come too late. Alice did not respond and, on 13 October, she died. Susan King was arrested and charged with manslaughter.

Susan's trial took place on 20 November 1871. After the child's mother, Annie Butcher had told her story, the prosecution called Edwin Merchan, who detailed his visit to Susan's home on 18 September. He was also able to confirm that, on his second visit, at 10.00pm, Susan had been under the influence of alcohol.

Dr Duckett, in addition to examining Alice and ordering her removal, had also performed the post-mortem, after the child had died. He reported that all of her internal organs were healthy, except for her lungs and brain. The lungs were badly inflamed and this was undoubtedly due to the poor treatment she had received. The cause of death was malnutrition, which had effected the lungs.

Eleanor Watson lived in the house next door to Susan, and had seen baby Alice when she had first arrived at the house. The child was healthy and robust then. Eleanor had only seen the child a couple of times since and by then she seemed to be very neglected. Eleanor had not, however, reported the matter to the police.

Susan King tried her best to say that Alice had been sickly ever since she had taken her from her mother. She had fed her well, and looked after her properly, but the child never seemed to recover and, despite her best efforts, became more and more ill. This did not, however, agree with the testimony of the other witnesses and the jury duly returned a verdict that Susan was guilty of manslaughter. She was then sentenced to eighteen months in prison.

# Chapter 16

# Lydia Venables
## 1872

Lydia Venables had lived with Alfred Chatterton for some sixteen months, by the time they moved into rooms at 67 Roman Road, Islington. Lydia, a widow, had lost her husband some three years before. Alfred, a man with a very short temper, had also been married, but wife had walked out on him at about the same time, as Lydia's husband died. Each of them brought a daughter to the new relationship. Alfred's daughter was now seven years old, whilst Lydia's daughter, Eliza, was three and a half. Lydia, though, doted on both children and was a good mother to them. Unfortunately, she was also rather fond of drink.

Though the children were never neglected, and always had enough to eat, there were times when Lydia would spend just a little too much of her housekeeping allowance on alcohol. This would cause arguments between her and Alfred, and sometimes these arguments ended in violence. There was also the fact that Alfred favoured his own child over Lydia's, and sometimes he beat Eliza. As a result, Lydia's daughter, Eliza, was rather frightened of her mother's new partner.

On Tuesday 13 August 1872, Alfred, a cab driver, went to work, as usual at around 8.00am. He did not return home, to Roman Road, until close to 5.00pm, to find that Lydia had gone out drinking, and there was no meal ready for him or the children. This made Alfred very angry indeed and he immediately went back out, looking for Lydia in all her usual haunts. Having failed to find any sign of her, Alfred returned to their lodgings at 6.00pm, and prepared something for him and the children to eat. Soon after finishing the meal, he went back out, but left a note for Lydia which, in no uncertain terms, told her exactly what he thought of her actions.

When Alfred went home again, at 8.30pm, he found Lydia waiting for him. She had obviously been drinking, though it could not be said that she was actually drunk. She had also read his curt note, and knew exactly what to expect now.

An argument broke out, which ended when Alfred slapped Lydia across the face, before announcing that he was going out for the night. It wasn't a very hard blow, but it was enough for Lydia to say: 'Perhaps you won't find me here when you get home.' To this, Alfred replied: 'And a very good job too, but mind you take your child with you.' That last phrase preyed on Lydia's mind, once Alfred had gone out. It was to lead to a terrible tragedy.

Eliza Giles also lodged at 67 Roman Road. She heard some of the argument between Lydia and Alfred, and heard him storm out, slamming the front door behind him. Soon afterwards, Lydia also left the house, but Eliza saw her return, a few minutes later, with a pot of beer. Then, for an hour or so, all seemed to be quiet.

At around 9.20pm, Eliza heard the elder girl, Alfred's daughter, scream and then shout: 'Oh mother, don't mother!' Eliza opened her front door and saw Lydia standing in the hallway. Lydia, seeing Eliza shouted: 'I have done it. I have done it. No one else has done it but me. Come in and see.'

Eliza walked into Lydia's rooms and saw that both girls were in their respective beds. Alfred's daughter sat bolt upright, a look of sheer terror on her face. As for little Eliza Venables, she lay in her cot, with her throat cut from ear to ear. Even as Eliza Giles looked upon this horrific scene, Lydia shouted: 'This is the knife I did it with. Didn't you hear me sharpening it on the poker?' Fearful of what Lydia might do to the other girl, Eliza Giles gathered the child into her arms and took her into her own rooms.

The scream had also been heard by Jane Simpson, the landlady of the house, who lived on the premises. She went upstairs, to see what the noise was all about, and found Lydia

Venables at her front door saying: 'Mrs Simpson, I have done it. She is happy now. Is she quite dead?'

The police, and a doctor were called. Constable John Vere found Lydia at the foot of her child's bed and, seeing the uniformed officer, Lydia remarked: 'I have killed my child. I will go with you. I will not run away.' She also told him that, what Alfred had said, had preyed on her mind, and she had feared that there would be no shelter for her, or her child. The only solution, in Lydia's eyes, had been to protect her daughter, by taking her life.

Eliza Venables was indeed dead. Dr Henry Straith was the medical gentleman called to the scene, and he noted that the child's throat had been cut down to the spine. Her head was almost severed from her body.

Charged with murder, Lydia Venables appeared at the Old Bailey on 19 August, just six days after she had killed her daughter. The prosecution case was outlined by Mr Ribton, whilst Lydia had two barristers to defend her: Mr Montagu Williams and Mr Straight.

There was no suggestion that Lydia's mind had been unbalanced at the time she took her child's life, and there was no doubt, with her repeated admissions, that she was responsible for killing Eliza. The jury, therefore, had little alternative but to return a verdict that she was guilty as charged, though they did add a strong recommendation to mercy. Sentenced to death, the jury's comments were taken to heart and Lydia's sentence was eventually commuted to a term of imprisonment.

# Chapter 17

# George Hannay Wilson
## 1873

**S**arah Wilson was a very worried woman. For some time now, her husband, George, had been behaving very erratically. So concerned had she become, that Sarah went to the local authorities, and asked if they could commit her husband to a mental asylum, so that he might get proper medical treatment.

The authorities had arranged for George to be examined by a doctor, and he confirmed that George was suffering from severe mental problems, and should be hospitalised without delay. There was, however, a problem. Before they would grant him a place at a suitable asylum, those same authorities insisted that Sarah must pay for two separate bonds of £100, against the treatment George would receive. There was absolutely no way that Sarah could find £200 in total and, though she appealed to the authorities, and begged them to reconsider, they would not hear of any reduction.

George Wilson had worked as an overseer in the letter sorting department of the Post Office, but had recently lost that job, again due to his increasingly strange behaviour. As a result, he now stayed at home all day, every day, at their house at 35 Catherine Street.

Things were no different from usual at 9.00am on Saturday 8 November 1873. George sat in the front parlour of the house, reading a newspaper. Sarah was in the kitchen, preparing her youngest son, ten-year-old Thomas, for school. The eldest boy, William, was naked, in a tin bath, soaking in the hot water. When he was almost ready, Thomas excused himself and went upstairs, briefly. It was when he came back down, as he passed the parlour door, close to the bottom of the stairs, that events took an horrific turn.

Without a word, George Hannay Wilson put down his newspaper, picked up a small axe, and grabbed hold of Thomas. A brutal blow was inflicted upon the child's head, and as Thomas fell to the floor, blood pouring from his injury, George knelt over his body, preparing to strike for a second time.

Sarah screamed at the top of her voice. This not only brought William Wilson to the scene, but also attracted the attention of Sarah's next door neighbour, James William Oxley.

James Oxley was about to have a wash himself, when the scream from next door caused him to rush out into the yard at the back of his house. Sarah Wilson was in the yard of number 35, and shouted: 'Come to my aid Mr Oxley. He has murdered my son.'

Throwing himself over the fence, between the two properties, James Oxley paused only to pick up a heavy broom as a weapon, before dashing into Sarah's house. He saw George, lifting the axe above his head, about to strike Thomas again, and a naked William wrestling with his father, and trying to pull him backwards. Oxley grabbed hold of George's right hand, the one that held the axe, and managed to pull him away from Thomas. George, though, still had hold of Thomas, with his left hand, and as George moved backwards, the boy was pulled along the corridor for a few feet.

James Oxley, and William Wilson, finally managed to subdue George, drag him back into the parlour and throw him down upon a couch. As James guarded him, William dressed quickly and ran off to fetch the police, and a doctor.

Dr Slater was at the house within a few minutes. Thomas was very badly injured and Dr Slater ordered that a cab should be called, and the child taken to hospital immediately. Thomas was still bleeding profusely from deep, incised wounds, just above his left temple, and it was clear that he had suffered an underlying fracture of the skull. The injuries proved to be far too severe, and later that morning, at 11.30am, Thomas Wilson died.

The inquest on the dead child opened at the *Lord Nelson*

public house, on Copenhagen Street, off Caledonian Road, on Monday 10 November. Sarah Wilson confirmed that, in the days since he had lost his job at the Post Office, her husband George had twice tried to commit suicide. As a result, all the razors in the house had been hidden, as Sarah had been fearful that George might harm himself. She had never thought that he might turn his attention towards his children.

The evidence having been heard by the jury, George was sent to face his trial for murder. That trial took place on 24 November, but there was only one witness. Dr John Rowland Gibson, who was the surgeon at Newgate prison, testified that George Wilson was of unsound mind, and therefore incapable of pleading to the indictment. Found guilty, but insane, George was sentenced to be detained during Her Majesty's pleasure. Finally, he was to receive the medical help that he so badly needed, but it had all come far too late for his son, Thomas, who had died for the lack of £200, needed to secure his father's treatment.

# Chapter 18

# William Cole
## 1876

**T**homas and Sabina Foy lived at 46 Payne Street, Islington, with their son, Peter. They also, occasionally, let out a room to a lodger. One such lodger was Eliza Stamp and, in June 1876, she moved to a new address, leaving some of her rent unpaid. So, when Eliza returned, on Saturday 10 June, to remove some items she had left behind, the Foys tried to prevent her from doing so. It was then that William Cole, who lived a couple of doors away, decided to intervene.

Cole told Thomas Foy to leave the woman alone and allow her to take away her own possessions. Foy told Cole that he would be better off minding his own business, and keeping his nose out of other peoples. Hearing that, William Cole offered to fight Foy, but the offer was declined. The matter was not, however, forgotten.

The following morning, Sunday 11 June, Sabina heard Cole shouting from outside: 'I have been waiting for you since five o clock.' Once again, Thomas Foy did not rise to the bait, but at 9.00am, Cole was at his front door with his sleeves rolled up and, seeing Sabrina in her kitchen, called out: 'You bloody Irish bitch, send out your bloody husband, and what I did not give him last night, I will give him this morning.' Some time after this, Thomas Foy appeared at his own door, his shirt off, ready to take on Cole.

The two men met in the middle of Payne Street, but it was Thomas Foy who struck the first blow, landing a punch on Cole's eye. Cole then grabbed hold of Foy, and the two men wrestled together until they fell to the ground. It was then that Thomas Foy's head struck the kerbstone, and he received a severe kick in the lower stomach. It was that kick, and the internal injuries it caused, which led to Foy's death later that same day. Cole was duly charged with manslaughter.

William Cole's trial took place on 8 August, and Sabrina Foy told the court about the interference and threats, which she had received from Cole. Her testimony was backed up by her son, Peter, and their lodger, Martha Frewin. All said that it had been Cole who had instigated the fight, and claimed that once they were on the floor together, Cole had kicked out, striking Foy hard in the lower stomach. Other witnesses, though, told a rather different story.

Robert Shellard lived at 7 Payne Street, and he described the fight as a fair fist-fight. If anything, Cole was at a disadvantage, as Foy was far bigger and stronger. As the two men fell to the floor, Shellard saw Sabrina Foy go forward, and kick Cole hard in his side. Shellard and other men then went to pull the two protagonoists off each other, but it was Foy who tried to pull free and rejoin the fight, at one stage shouting to Cole: 'Have you had enough?' Finally, Shellard was able to state that whilst Foy was a known drunkard in the area, Cole was a teetotaller and had a good character.

Joseph Mitchell lived next door to the Foys, and he was in a good position to hear what passed between Sabrina Foy and William Cole, before the fight started. He heard Sabrina using all sorts of foul and disgusting language against Cole. Mitchell had also seen Sabrina kick out two or three times once her husband was on the ground, and said that those kicks might have been received by either of the two men.

The final witness was Constable George Horsford, the officer who had taken Cole into custody after Foy had died. On the way to the police station Foy had remarked: 'We had a fight, but I did not kick. If Foy was kicked, I believe it was intended for me.' Later, Cole claimed that he had received a kick himself, but he could not say who had inflicted it. What was certain is that he was in no position to kick out and even if he had, he was wearing soft shoes at the time. Horsford ended by confirming that the prisoner was a most industrious, quiet and sober man.

The jury decided that William Cole had not inflicted the kick that led to Thomas Foy's death, and returned a verdict that he was innocent of the charge against him. It was, of course, likely that the kick had actually been administered by Sabrina Foy, but there was insufficient evidence to charge her with any offence.

# Chapter 19

# Charles Cornish
# 1877

O n Saturday 16 June 1877, William Cornish returned to his home at 498 Liverpool Road, to find his wife in a state of complete hysteria. For some time she was unable to say anything to him, but eventually managed to gasp out that their son, twenty-nine-year-old Charles, had run off. William gently asked his wife why Charles had run away, but again she was unable to give him any details. All she could do, was to tell William to go upstairs.

William, by now an extremely worried man, walked gingerly upstairs and into the bedroom that Charles shared with his wife, Hannah and their daughter, Hannah Louisa. There he found the reason for his wife's state of acute agitation for there, on the bed, lay the body of ten-year-old Hannah Louisa Cornish, her throat cut deeply from ear to ear.

William ran to find a policeman and returned to the house, at 11.30pm, with Constable Cohen. He checked the bedroom, which was in the front room on the first floor, and confirmed for himself the terrible scene within. William Cornish was then despatched to fetch a doctor and returned a few minutes later, with Dr George White.

As Dr White examined the tragic bundle on the bloodstained bed, Charles Cornish entered the room. Constable Cohen demanded to know if Charles had a knife on him and received the one word answer: 'No.' Informed that he would be taken to the police station, Charles then asked: What for? I have done nothing.

Charles Cornish faced his trial on 1 July 1877. The first witness was Constable Cohen, who testified that when Charles first came into the room where his daughter's body lay, he appeared to be very agitated indeed. He seemed to be unaware that anything was amiss and could see no reason why the police and a doctor were present.

In addition to telling the court of his wife's agitation when he returned home on 16 June, William Cornish, the prisoner's father, said that his son had behaved very erratically of late. Some months before, William had sent Charles to an asylum, where he had stayed for seven weeks, receiving treatment for his mental problems. Upon his release, William had offered a room to Charles, his wife and his daughter, so that he could help supervise him and protect him.

Millie Ganderson, although she was only twelve years old, acted as a nurse and helper to Cornish's family. She testified that at about 10.00pm on 16 June, the prisoner had come into the living room and asked her where his wife was. Millie told him that she had gone out, whereupon Charles went into the front room, where his daughter slept. Five minutes later, Charles came back out to tell Millie that his daughter was asleep. The suggestion was that in those few minutes, Charles had cut Hannah's throat, for he left the house again soon afterwards.

Charles's wife, Hannah Maria Cornish, stepped into the witness box to give her testimony and immediately fainted. She was carried from the court and did not recover enough to ever tell the court what she knew.

The last two witnesses were both medical gentlemen. Dr White told of his visit to the house and confirmed that the child's throat was cut so deeply that the wound had penetrated down to the spine. Later he had examined a somewhat dazed Charles Cornish who again repeated: 'What have I done?' He kept on saying that as the examination continued.

The final witness was Dr J R Gibson, the surgeon from Newgate prison. He said that he had had Cornish under observation since he had arrived at the prison and was of the opinion that he was insane now, and had been in the same condition at the time he took his daughter's life, and so was not responsible for his actions.

The jury chose to accept that opinion and returned the verdict that Charles Cornish was guilty of murder, but insane. He was then sentenced to be detained until Her Majesty's pleasure be made known.

# Chapter 20

# John Lynch

## 1877

n November 1868, John Lynch married Bridget Carmody and soon afterwards the couple moved to Brighton, residing in Russell Street. John carried on his business, as a tailor, and together they had four children over the next few years. Then, on 30 June 1877, tragedy struck the family when the youngest child, also named John, died.

The death of her new-born son greatly affected Bridget Lynch. She became depressed and grew apart from her husband. He, in his turn, could not believe that the death of a child had driven such a wedge between man and wife and managed to convince himself that Bridget must be having an affair with a man she knew, who worked at the Brighton Aquarium. John Lynch took to drinking rather more than usual and, when he was under the influence of alcohol, he often beat Bridget. This drove them even further apart until eventually, Bridget decided that enough was enough. Taking her three children with her, she left John and moved to London, staying at various addresses, but finally lodging with her uncle and aunt, John and Alice Carmody, in Islington. This move to London only served to convince John Lynch that he had been correct all along. His wife had been having an affair with the man from the aquarium.

On Monday 30 July 1877, Bridget and her aunt, Alice, decided to go for a walk together. When the two ladies returned to the house, they found John Lynch waiting for them. Lynch seemed to be calm enough and Alice thought it would be a good idea to leave the two in private to talk through their problems. Minutes later, however, Bridget's eldest child rushed in to announce: 'Dadda is beating mamma.'

Alice and John Carmody went to investigate and found Lynch beating his wife. At one stage, as she tried to escape around a bed, Lynch kicked violently at her. John Carmody wasted no time in running to find a police officer.

Constable George Davenport soon arrived at the house, restrained Lynch, and put him out into the street. The officer then asked the Carmodys if they wished to prefer charges against Lynch, but they agreed that they did not wish there to be any further trouble. Lynch was sent on his way, with a severe warning from Constable Davenport.

In fact, Lynch did return to the house, some ten minutes later. There were more harsh words exchanged and at one stage Lynch lashed out at John Carmody. The threat of calling the policeman back seemed to have the desired effect, though, and Lynch finally left the house, saying that he wouldn't bother the family again.

For the next few days, all was well, but then, on Sunday 5 August, Bridget received a note, delivered by a young boy. The note was from Lynch and seemed to be a contrite apology for his recent behaviour. It went on to ask Bridget to meet him, so that they might go for a peaceful walk and talk through their differences. Bridget wanted to go, but was fearful of further violence, no matter what her husband had written. To calm those fears, Alice Carmody said she would go with Bridget and the two women left the house some time around noon.

It was around 12.30pm when Bridget and Alice met Lynch in Green Man Road. Lynch was very calm indeed and spoke most pleasantly to his wife. The three then went for a short walk, during which no words of anger were used and no hints of violence made. They walked down Essex Road, into River Street and on into Marquess Road. It all seemed to be going well and then Lynch even invited the two ladies to join him for a drink, in the *Marquess Tavern*.

Lynch bought himself an Irish whisky and paid for a lemonade for each of the two ladies. Lynch was still behaving impeccably and, after some hours in the public house, they left and returned to Canonbury Road. To make conversation, Bridget asked her husband if he had anyone waiting for him. He replied that Patsy and Martin, his two brothers, were nearby, and invited Bridget to go with him to meet them. She replied that she didn't really want to, to which Lynch commented: 'Come along. Don't be disagreeable. There will be no row. You will be all right.'

A somewhat reluctant Bridget met the two brothers further down the road and the entire party then returned to the *Marquess Tavern*. Still Lynch was on his best behaviour and the couple even discussed renting a room together, somewhere in the West End. Lynch wanted this to happen immediately but Bridget said she would rather wait until the following day, Monday 6 August.

It was around 7.30pm when Bridget, Alice, Lynch and his two brothers, finally left the *Marquess*. Everyone still appeared to be on the friendliest of terms, as they walked down Canonbury Road to the junction with Essex Road. It was there, for the first time, that the atmosphere changed somewhat.

Lynch was still insisting that Bridget should come with him right away. Alice Carmody, concerned at this, suggested that Bridget should come home with her immediately. Finally, after some discussion, Lynch agreed to meet his wife at 10.30am the following morning. He then hailed a Hansom cab but then, rather curiously, asked Bridget to get into the cab with him.

Even before Bridget could reply, Patrick Lynch, known as Patsy, warned Bridget: 'Johnny has got a razor in his pocket.' Lynch immediately denied this and joked that his brother was always telling lies. At that point, Patrick and Martin Lynch both climbed into the cab, leaving Bridget, her husband, and Alice Carmody on the street nearby.

Bridget, now rather concerned, asked Lynch if he did indeed have a razor in his pocket and if he had meant to use it on her inside the cab. Again Lynch denied that there was any truth in what his brother had said. Bridget then asked if she might take a look for herself and said that she would look in his pocket. She put out her hand, as if to go into Lynch's pocket and he half-turned from her. Then, in an instant, he drew something from his pocket and there was a flash of light close to Bridget's neck.

Immediately blood spurted from Bridget's throat. She fell into a sitting position on the kerb and managed to cry out: 'Oh aunt! I am killed.' Seeing the ever widening pool of blood around her niece, Alice Carmody screamed as loudly as she could.

That scream was heard by a police officer on duty nearby. By coincidence, that officer was Constable George Davenport, the man who had ejected Lynch from the house a few days previously. By the time he reached the scene of the attack, Bridget had slumped onto her back. Lynch was still standing nearby and, once he was named as the attacker by those nearby, Davenport arrested him.

Another officer, Constable William Butcher, had also heard the scream and rushed to the corner of Essex Road. He saw that Lynch was being held by Davenport, who did not seem to require any assistance, so Butcher ran to fetch Dr Huggin whose surgery was nearby, at 29 Canonbury Road. By the time the doctor arrived, Bridget was dead and Lynch was now facing a charge of wilful murder.

John Lynch's trial took place on 17 September 1877, before Mr Justice Hawkins. The case for the Crown was led by Mr Poland, assisted by Mr Straight. Lynch was defended by Mr Montagu Williams.

In addition to the witnesses already mentioned, the prosecution called Dr Samuel Tilcot Huggin, who said he had been called to the corner of Essex Road by Constable Butcher. He timed his arrival there at close to 8.00pm on 5 August. He saw a woman lying on the pavement, a deep gash in her throat. Her larynx was severed and blood was just ceasing to flow from the left carotid artery. She was already dead.

Emily Newton had been in Essex Road at the time of the attack upon Bridget. She had seen a group of people standing near a cab. Emily was only a few yards away when she saw Bridget go to feel inside Lynch's pocket. He turned away for the briefest of moments and then seemed to strike Bridget in the throat.

Inspector John Rowland Jamieson had been the officer in charge of the Islington police station on the day in question. It was some time after 8.00pm when Lynch was brought in. He had been drinking, but was certainly not drunk. He was searched and, in his left-hand coat pocket, Jamieson found an empty razor case. He also found a piece of official looking paper and even as he opened it, Lynch had said: 'You will find a notice there from my wife. I asked her to settle it, but she would not.' The paper was a summons to appear in court at the Guildhall, on Wednesday 8 August, for an earlier assault upon Bridget.

Placed into a cell, Lynch seemed to show no concern over his predicament, immediately going off to sleep. When he awoke, he asked if his wife were dead. Told that she was he cried a little and then said: 'I hope she is in Heaven.'

Inspector Jamieson also detailed a comment Lynch had made when he stood before the magistrates at the police court. Turning to look at Bridget's uncle, John Carmody, he had shouted: 'You see Jack. I have had my satisfaction. This will teach you to harbour a man's wife and children. This is all through you. You dirty old wretch. It was you that kept her away from me and I am very glad that she is dead.'

Patrick Lynch, the prisoner's brother, told the court that he lived at 4 Upper Rupert Street, in Haymarket. At 10.30am, Lynch had called at his house and shown him a new razor in its case. Martin Lynch had also seen this razor and heard his brother remark that he wanted to send his three children to the workhouse.

This behaviour seemed to indicate that the entire crime had been premeditated. This appeared to be confirmed by the testimony of the final witness, John Selby Perry. He worked as an assistant at a cutler's shop owned by Mr Davis. Perry testified that on the morning of Saturday 4 August, Lynch had called into the shop and purchased a new razor for one shilling. That razor had stamped upon it: J.C. Davis, 69 Leadenhall Street, as had the one found at the scene of the crime, proving that it was the one Lynch had used to kill his wife the very next day.

Found guilty of murder and sentenced to death, twenty-six-year-old John Lynch paid the ultimate penalty on Monday 15 October 1877, when he was hanged at Newgate prison by William Marwood.

# Chapter 21

# Thomas Neal
# 1890

Although Thomas Neal lived with his wife, Theresa, at 81 St Peter Street, in Islington, they had a habit of breakfasting each morning with Theresa's mother, Esther Elizabeth Gray, who lived close by.

On Tuesday 28 January 1890, Thomas Neal called at his mother-in-law's house, as usual, a few minutes after 9.00am. Esther asked where Theresa was and Thomas replied that she would be along directly. First, however, he had a job to do and, as he said that, he picked up a hammer from the fireplace, and left, telling Esther that he would return with Theresa very soon. The hammer, which Thomas had taken with him, as one that he had left it at Esther's house a few days previously. Esther thought nothing of this and carried on preparing the breakfast.

Time passed and still there was no sign of Thomas and Theresa so Esther Gray sent her son, Henry, to find out what was delaying them. He returned, a few minutes later, to say that something terrible seemed to have happened, and there was now a large crowd of people outside Theresa's home in St Peter Street. He then added: 'Tessie is lying in a pool of blood in the street.'

Esther went to investigate, for herself and saw, on her arrival at St Peter Street, that a crowd had gathered around a figure, who was lying on the pavement. As she drew closer, Esther saw, to her horror, that the stricken figure was indeed her daughter, Theresa Neal, who had been beaten about the neck and then stabbed in the head. Meanwhile, a police search had been launched for Thomas, who neighbours had seen walking away from the scene. He was eventually arrested, that night, and charged with murdering his wife.

Thomas Neal's trial for murder took place at the Old Bailey on 8 March 1890, before the Lord Chief Justice, Lord Coleridge. At the outset it was explained to the court that, whilst the prisoner was sixty-four-years-old, his wife was much younger. They had married in 1883, when she was just eighteen, and he was fifty-seven, and since that date, she had borne him five children. At the time of her death, Theresa was only twenty-five, almost forty years her husband's junior.

Eliza Waterman was the landlady of the house at 81 St Peter Street, and lived on the premises. She testified that a man, and his wife came to her house on the Friday before Theresa was attacked, that is, 24 January. They appeared to be a most respectable couple and said they wished to rent the front room on the second floor.

That same evening, a strange man called and asked for the front door key, explaining that he had taken the front room. Eliza was suspicious and told him that he was not the man she had rented the room to that morning. He explained that he was Thomas Neal and that the man who had called earlier was his brother and had rented the room on his behalf. Eliza was not happy with the situation, but after some argument, she finally handed the key over. Later that night, Theresa arrived and the couple started living together.

On Monday 29 January, Eliza had seen Theresa for the first time. The new tenant was carrying some furniture downstairs and Eliza demanded to know what was going on. After all, this was not the woman to whom she had rented the room in the first place. Theresa explained to Eliza who she was, and told her that she was married to Thomas. She also confirmed that it had been her sister-in-law, and her husband, who had taken the room on their behalf.

Turning to the fact that furniture was being moved, Eliza asked Theresa if they were thinking of moving yet again. Theresa replied that they simply had too much furniture in the room and she was going to sell some of it. Eliza had no objection. After all, the furniture did belong to Thomas and Theresa, as they had rented the room unfurnished.

The next time Eliza had heard anything concerning her new tenants, was at 9.30am on the Tuesday, when she heard a loud screaming coming from the upstairs room. Eliza dashed upstairs to be met by Theresa, who was on her way down, dressed only in her nightdress and bleeding badly from a wound in her face. At this point, Thomas Neal appeared from his room and pushed past the two women, saying: 'They've robbed me enough.'

When Esther Gray, the dead woman's mother, gave her testimony, a possible motive for this crime was revealed. Esther began by outlining the events of the morning of Tuesday 28 January, when Thomas called for the hammer and said he would be back soon with Theresa.

Esther went on to say that the previous October, Thomas had received a sentence of two months' imprisonment for cutting her head. Apparently they had argued and Thomas had lashed out at Esther, with a stick, causing a wound to her head. During the time that he was incarcerated, Theresa had taken lodgings with a friend of theirs, a man named Harry Day. Whilst Esther did not believe that there had been any intimacy between her daughter and Day, Thomas Neal was sure that there had been. As a result, ever since his release from prison he had behaved differently towards his wife.

Edward Beesley was another friend of the family and, ever since Thomas had been sent to prison for assault, he had had care of their three surviving children, two having died in infancy. He also knew Harry Day and had spoken to Thomas about his wife having had to live with Day, whilst he was in jail. At no time had Thomas mentioned to him that he had any suspicions over Theresa's behaviour, and no intimacy with Day was ever suggested.

Anne March lived in Parkfield Street and, before they had moved to St Peter Street, the Neals had lodged with her. She testified that she had heard Thomas arguing with his wife about her relationship with Day, and had once accused her of going to see a show at the Britannia Theatre with him. Theresa had denied this, but Thomas was not to be convinced, and swore that he would put a knife right through her if he ever had the proof as to what had taken place.

Mrs Holloway lived next door to the Neals, at 83 St Peter Street, and she said that she had heard a dreadful screaming coming from next door on the morning of 28 January. She had picked up a poker and hammered on the wall to shut the neighbours up, but this nothing to quieten them. Moments later she heard a woman's voice shout: 'Oh, don't kill me. You know I love you. I love you with all my heart.'

Police witnesses detailed Thomas Neal's arrest. Constable Charles Huntley told the court how he had seen Neal in a tobacconist's shop, on the Balls Pond Road and taken him to the police station for interview. Once he had been charged with his wife's murder, Neal's only comment was: 'Put me in a warm cell.'

Thomas Neal's defence was that he had been sorely provoked by his wife, especially over her affair with Harry Day, and though he was responsible for taking her life, this provocation should reduce the charge to one of manslaughter. The jury did not agree and Neal was found guilty. Asked if he had anything to say before the sentence of death was given, Neal replied: 'I'm sorry I committed the murder, but she was a bad wife to me.'

Thomas Neal, a small, grey-haired man with large features, did pay the ultimate penalty for his crime, being hanged at Newgate prison, on 26 March 1890, by James Berry.

# Chapter 22

# Walter Alfred Hargan
## 1890

For some time, there had been trouble, at the *Wagon and Horses* public house on Hertford Road. The house had always had a reputation as a lower-class establishment, with a coarse clientele, but now, at last, things were beginning to change.

In the early part of 1890, a new landlord, Thomas Peck, had been appointed, and he determined, that the place should be improved. He would not stand for any misbehaviour, or trouble and, slowly, he began to persuade many of the regular troublemakers to find somewhere else to drink. This approach, however, had consequences, in that some of the more rowdy customers, objected to Peck's methods and tried to make things as difficult as possible for him.

Early on the afternoon of Wednesday 30 July 1890, Thomas Peck went up to his bedroom. He was exhausted from his efforts of the previous evening, and decided to have a lie down on his bed. Moments later, Thomas was asleep, meaning that his wife, Jane Harriett, was left on her own in the bar.

At 2.00pm, four men entered the *Wagon and Horses*. They were William Lambert, Charles George Jones, John Wheeler and a man named Gray, and all four were known troublemakers. For more than two hours, the four men were rowdy and abusive. Though differing stories would later be told in court, the upshot was that at one stage, a customer in one of the other bars, a man named Walter Alfred Hargan, walked behind the bar, and brandished a revolver at the men, telling them to be quiet.

As Jane Harriett Peck gently pushed Hargan back into the other bar, three of the four men became even more obnoxious. Jones, Wheeler and Lambert all began singing lustily, and dancing. They used the foulest language towards Jane, and tried to get behind the bar themselves. Finally, at one particularly difficult time, Jane screamed out for help. That scream woke her husband Thomas, who immediately ran downstairs to see what the problem was.

With some difficulty, Thomas Peck managed to eject all three troublemakers, and then bolted the front door against them. They then stood outside, shouting further abuse. In all the confusion, no-one saw Hargan leave, by the back door.

A number of witnesses saw what happened next. Hargan began walking slowly down Hertford Road, towards Downham Road. Then, suddenly, the three men who had been thrown out of the pub saw the man who had brandished a gun at them, and decided that they would deal with him. They began to follow him down Hertford Road, and one of them shouted for him to turn around.

Hargan stopped, and turned around slowly. He saw the three men, still walking quickly towards him, but said nothing. He simply turned back, and continued walking away. Once again, the three shouted for him to stop. It was obvious that they were intent of causing further trouble, but Hargan had had enough.

Once again, Hargan turned but this time he took the revolver out of his pocket. He pointed the weapon towards the three men, but it did not stop them coming towards him. A shot was fired into the air but still Lambert, Wheeler and Jones continued to advance on Hargan. Then, very quickly, two more shots were fired. First, William Lambert fell, to be followed seconds later by John Wheeler. Charles Jones also fell but, whereas the other two men had been hit, Jones was merely trying to persuade Hargan that he had been wounded so that he would not fire again. Hargan, seeing all three men on the ground, took a step forward and said: 'Lie down there dead you bastards', before putting the gun back into his pocket, and walking away.

There were a number of people in and around Hertford Road who had either heard, or seen, the shooting, and they now began to follow Hargan. At first they didn't get too close. This man had, after all, just shot two men, and still had the weapon in his

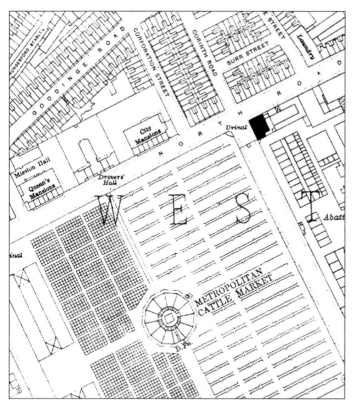

A map showing the location of the *Lion Tavern*, where Charles Bricknell stabbed Jane Gary to death. Author's collection

How the *Illustrated Police News* showed the murder of Theresa Neal, by her husband, Thomas. Author's collection

George Chapman, the man found guilty of poisoning three women, two of them in Islington. Author's collection

THE PENALTY OF HIS CRIMES.

How the newspapers of the day portrayed the execution of Chapman. Note how he has to be supported on the trap.
Author's collection

Part of the statement written by Arthur Canham, explaining how he had killed his wife, Selina, and then tried to take his own life.
The National Archives

Rosina Field, the woman murdered at the furniture shop where Murphy worked.
The National Archives

Inside the furniture warehouse at 22 Islington Green, where Frederick Murphy worked. The National Archives

The mysterious note which Murphy sent to Stanley Wilton, explaining that there was a body in the shop's cellar. The National Archives

Dear Stan
dont get frigtln there is a dead women in no 22 and you can beluved me Stan it nothing to do with me but you know what the police will say it was me for sure but if they take the trouble to find out where I was all the time what they wont take the trouble to do, Stan I cant write I so upset about it.

Stan you can belived nt dont know any thing about how this women got in the celler of no 22

Rosina's body, in the cellar at
22 Islington Green.
The National Archives

Catherine Peck,
also nicknamed
Rose, the first
woman Murphy
had been accused
of killing.
The National Archives

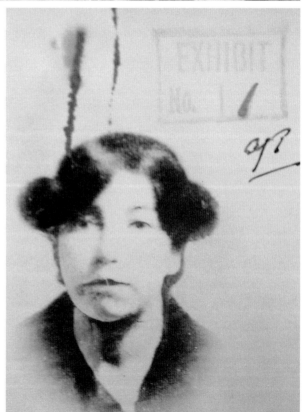

The old shelter, opposite Hall's Tobacconist's shop in Tollington Way. The National Archives

The body of Ronald James Marley, as it was found inside the air-raid shelter. The National Archives

The alleyway, where Michael Xinaris killed James Robinson. The National Archives

A mortuary picture of James Robinson, showing the wounds he had suffered.
The National Archives

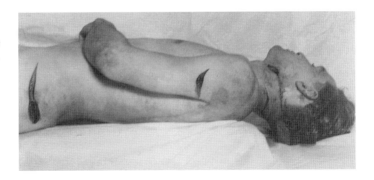

Seven Sisters Road, where Constable Summers was stabbed by Ronald Henry Marwood. The
National Archives

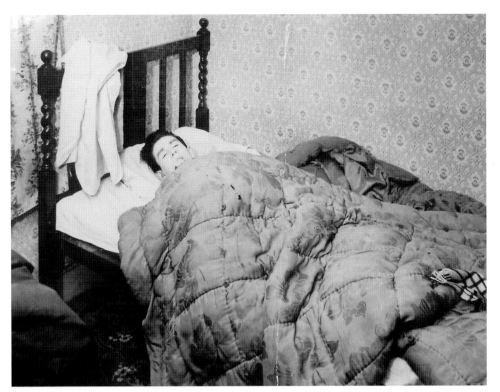

The body of Michael Joseph Teahan in his bed. The National Archives

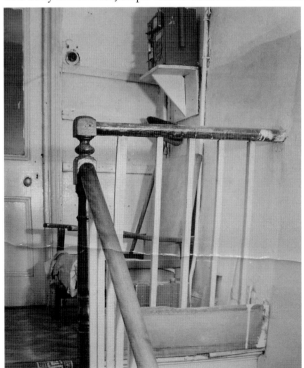

The new gas meter at Andover Road. The National Archives

Sofronis Café at 162 Seven Sisters Road, outside which Panayotis Gregorgiou shot Costas Vassiliou. The National Archives

Another police photograph of the murder scene. The National Archives

The bloodstains outside the café. The National Archives

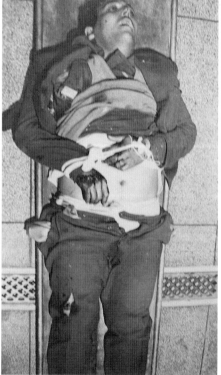

The body of Costas Vassiliou, in the mortuary. The National Archives

pocket. Some of the people threw stones at him. Others told him to come back, and wait for the police. Occasionally, Hargan drew the gun out again, and threatened to shoot anyone who came too close but, eventually, as the people drew ever closer, a couple of men managed to grab Hargan and take the gun from him. Now the mob grew more confidant, and some began to assault Hargan. One even brought a rope, and placed it around his neck. It was, possibly, only the arrival of the police, that saved Hargan's life.

It soon became clear that whilst Charles Jones was uninjured, both of the other men were dead. Taken into custody, Walter Hargan found himself charged with two murders. He appeared at the Old Bailey on 8 September 1890, when only evidence relating to the charge of killing William Lambert was heard. The case for the prosecution was detailed by Mr Horace Avory and Mr Muir. Hargan was defended by Mr Geoghegan and Mr Lever.

The first witness was the sole survivor of the shooting, Charles George Jones. He, quite naturally, told a story that painted him, and his companions, as largely innocent of any troublemaking. It was true that they were all singing and dancing, but they were not doing anyone any harm. Jane Peck, the wife of the landlord, had objected to their merrymaking, and tried to throw them out of the pub. At one stage she had said: 'I have got somebody in the other bar to protect me.' Mrs Peck had then brought Hargan behind the bar, and he had threatened them with his revolver.

Soon after this, since the men had still refused to leave the pub, Mrs Peck had struck Jones in the face. This had caused such an argument, that Mr Peck had come downstairs and thrown Lambert and Wheeler out into the street. Jones had not been ejected, but had simply left when his friends were put out. Later, in the street, they saw Hargan, and as they walked off in the same direction, towards Downham Road, he turned and without warning fired three shots.

Jane Peck told a rather different story. She had suffered almost two hours of abuse at the hands of Jones and his friends. Their language had been the most foul and abusive she could imagine, and at one stage, it had been Lambert who had lashed out and hit her in the face. Her scream had brought her husband downstairs, and he had put the men outside. As for asking Hargan to protect her, she had done no such thing.

Thomas Peck knew nothing of the problems in the bar downstairs, until he heard his wife scream. Going down he found Lambert trying to force his way into the private part of the house. Thomas told him that he wasn't allowed in there, and pointed out that the dog was loose, and would certainly bite him if he came through. Thomas then managed to force Lambert out into the street, and then immediately did the same with Wheeler. Jones did not leave of his own accord, but also had to be put out and tried to strike Thomas, as he left.

Having locked the door against the three troublemakers, Thomas then saw them run past the window, heading towards Downham Road. He then went outside to see what they were up to, and saw them confront Hargan as he stood outside a baker's shop at the end of the street. Three shots were then fired in rapid succession. The first had no effect, the second caused Lambert to fall and the third hit Wheeler.

Dennis Cockerell was in the *Wagon and Horses*, with a friend of his, Alfred Ongar. They testified that Mrs Peck had not, at any stage, asked Hargan for help. At one stage during the trouble, Hargan had walked behind the bar, without permission, and showed the three men that he had a revolver. He did not threaten the men and, once she had seen him, Mrs Peck gently pushed him back behind the counter.

George Brown had been in Hertford Road, and saw Hargan walking towards him. He then saw three men come out of the *Wagon and Horses*, and follow Hargan down the street. Brown saw the subsequent shooting, and was one of the men who then followed Hargan along Downham Road, and finally seized hold of him.

Another witness to the shooting was Frederick Ramsay who had a bootmaker's shop at 34 Hertford Road. This was almost directly opposite to the baker's shop, where the shooting took place, so Ramsay had a perfect view of the events, through his shop window. He also testified that it had been the three men who challenged Hargan, and were intent on causing him harm.

George Turner was a fishmonger, his shop being a few doors down from the *Wagon and Horses*. At the time of the shooting, George had been standing at his front door. After Hargan had fired the three shots, he placed his hands in his pocket and walked calmly away.

Constable John Cochrane was on duty close to Hertford Road, and heard the sound of shooting. Rushing to the scene he found two men lying dead on the pavement, close to the baker's shop. Cochrane, was one of the officers who rescued Hargan from the mob. He was also able to confirm that the two dead men, and Jones, were all well known to the police, and had a number of convictions for violence, drunkenness, fighting and assault.

Constable William Oakley was another officer, who ran to Hertford Road when he heard the sound of shooting. He found Hargan being held by a large group of people, and could see that he had already been badly assaulted. If anything, Hargan seemed relieved to be taken into custody.

At the police station, the gun Hargan had used, was examined by Sergeant Richard Mercer. He found that it was a six-shot revolver. Three chambers were now empty, but the other three were still loaded with live bullets.

The final witness was Dr John Herd Gordon, who had been brought to Hertford Road by the police. He confirmed that both Lambert and Wheeler were dead. Lambert had a bullet wound on the right side of his head whilst Wheeler had a wound to the left side of his right ear. Both had been physically very large, strong men in life.

There could be no doubt that Walter Hargan had shot two men dead, but the jury also took into account that he had left the *Wagon and Horses*, and was on his way home to his lodgings at 5 Southgate Road, when he was stopped by three men intent on doing him injury. Those same men had already been ejected from a public house, for causing trouble, and all had criminal records for violence and other offences. It was those facts which caused the jury to return a verdict that Hargan was not guilty of the murder of William Lambert, but was guilty of his manslaughter.

There was still the case of the shooting of John Wheeler to answer. Asked how he wished to plead, Hargan said that he was not guilty of murder, but again guilty of manslaughter. The prosecution accepted that plea and offered no evidence on the murder charge.

For those two offences of manslaughter, Walter Hargan was sentenced to twenty years' imprisonment, both sentences to run concurrently.

# Chapter 23

# Alfred Gamble
## 1895

George Henry Dowling and his wife, Ellen, had been happily married for a number of years and now had a family of nine children, the youngest of whom was Sidney Victor Dowling, who, in October 1895, was two years and three months old. The Dowlings lived at 42 Parkfield Street, off Liverpool Road, in Islington and were well liked by all of their neighbours.

On Thursday 8 October, George Dowling left for work as usual, and all the children went off to school, leaving just Ellen and Sidney alone in the house. Ellen had things to do about the house, and needed a way to keep Sidney amused for an hour or so. It was a pleasant enough day, so Ellen took her son across the road to the shop run by Jessie Murphy. A small bag of dates was purchased, and Ellen then returned to her own house. Sidney liked to sit on the front step of the house, and watch the world go by, so Ellen left him there, with his dates, being careful to leave the front door open so she could keep an eye on him. It was then just after 9.45am.

After a couple of minutes, Sidney went back into the house, and kindly offered one of the juicy dates to his mother. She thanked him, and accepted the gift, whereupon a happy Sidney skipped back down the hallway, and resumed his position on the step.

A few minutes later, Sidney was back, and now he held a very large pear, that he said someone had given to him. Ellen noticed that there was a small blemish on one part of the fruit, so took a sharp kitchen knife and cut it off. She then handed the pear back to Sidney who, happy with his prize, went back to the front step. At about this time, Jessie Murphy looked out of her shop window, and saw Sidney, his legs dangling over the step, eating the pear.

At around 10.20am, Harriett Willoughby, a seventeen-year-old servant girl, who lived next door to one to the Dowlings, at number 40, went to the water closet in the yard of her house. It was whilst she was in there that she heard a loud clattering sound and, going out to investigate, saw that someone had thrown a sack on top of the dustbin at the back of the house. Taking a closer look, Harriett saw that there was something in the sack; something which appeared to be some sort of mannequin.

Harriett immediately went back into number 40, and told her master, Mr Ebenezer Kurn, that someone had dumped a wax dummy, or something similar, on top of their dustbin. A curious Mr Kurn went to see for himself, but discovered, to his horror, that what had actually been dumped, was the body of a child. Kurn felt the body and found it was still warm. As he gently carried the bundle into his house, he told Harriett to run as fast as she could to find a policeman and a doctor.

As a tearful Harriett Willoughby ran out into the street, she almost bumped in to Ellen Dowling. Ellen asked her why she was crying and Harriett sobbed: 'The master has sent me for a policeman, for there is a baby found in our dust-hole.' A few minutes before this, Harriett had gone to her own front door, to check up on her son, and discovered that he was no longer on the step. At first, she had thought that he had simply wandered off, but now she exclaimed: 'Good God, it can"t be mine!'

At that moment, Elenezer Kurn appeared at his front door and, hearing what Ellen had just said, confirmed that they had found the body of a young child. He then invited her to come and inspect the tragic bundle for herself, to see if it was her missing son. A nervous Ellen stepped into Kurn's house, and saw that her worst fears were confirmed. There, on a sack, lay the naked body of her son Sidney.

By 10.45am, Dr Bertram Goddard was in attendance at number 40. By this time, attempts had been made to revive Sidney, by warming him, giving him drops of brandy, and applying gentle pressure to his chest, but no signs of life had been found. Dr Goddard examined the boy, and confirmed that life was extinct. He was also able to determine a probable cause of death. Though confirmation would have to wait until after the post-mortem had been carried out, Dr Goddard found that about an ounce of paper had been forced deep into Sidney's mouth and throat, thus cutting off his air supply. When the pieces were removed, they were seen to be portions of the *Daily Telegraph*, for 12 September.

The police already had a number of clues to go on. First, the fact that the body had been dumped onto the dustbin of number 40, indicated that it may well have been thrown over a wall of one of the adjacent houses. Secondly, the pieces of newspaper removed from Sidney's throat had been ripped into small squares, indicating that they might well have been prepared for use as toilet paper in one of the outside lavatories. Officers decided to search all the adjacent houses and dustbins.

The Dowlings lived at number 42, the Kurns lived at 40, and so the initial search concentrated on the house between them, number 41. Quite a number of people lived at that address. The owner was Mrs Burgess, a lady who ran a number of fruit stalls in the vicinity. Amongst the other people living there was Joseph Hampston, Mrs Burgess brother, who worked for her. Also living in the house was George Irons, Henry William Hurdle, George Hallicar and twelve-year-old George Miles, who was Mrs Burgess' grandson. Unfortunately for the police, though, every single one of those people had been out of the house that morning, and all had witnesses as to their whereabouts at the time of the murder. Nevertheless, the police felt that a search of that house was called for.

The search of number 41 was carried out by Constable Mason and Sergeant Thomas. They were accompanied by Joseph Hampston, who acted as a guide around the premises. The search was immediately fruitful. In the outside water-closet, Mason found a small, fur-lined cape which was instantly identified by Ellen Dowling, as one which Sidney had been wearing. Then, in the dustbin of the same house, Sergeant Thomas found a child's pinafore, a shirt, a pair of drawers and a frock, all of which belonged to Sidney, and which he had been wearing that day. Finally, as if further proof that someone at number 41 might well have been responsible for the crime, portions of the *Daily Telegraph*, of the same date as those found in Sidney's throat, were found inside the water closet. The inference was clear: Sidney Dowling had been murdered in the water closet of number 41.

A shocked Joseph Hampston exclaimed: 'Good God, I am innocent.' The officers who heard that felt that it was a most curious thing to say, as he had not been accused of any involvement in the crime. Hampston was taken into custody but, once his alibi had been checked, he was released, later that same day.

That evening, though, a new suspect's name came to the attention of the police. Mrs Burgess had explained that whilst her house had been empty all day, there had been two visitors at about the time that Sidney had been taken. She had been to the fruit market very early that day and, having made her purchases, she told her brother, Joseph Hampston, to take a cart and store some of the items at number 41. Joseph had indeed driven the cart, to the address, but he had had a young assistant with him, and it had been that assistant who was left alone at the house, and had unloaded the cart, whilst Joseph returned to the fruit stall in Chapel Street. The name of that assistant was Alfred Gamble.

Alfred Gamble was not an imposing figure. Sixteen years of age, tall and thin, he was usually dressed quite scruffily. He suffered from severe deafness and was also rather slow-witted. He had also been the only person who had stepped foot inside number 41 that morning, had been the only one with the keys at the crucial time and, when interviewed, admitted giving Sidney the pear, though he denied any involvement in his murder. Nevertheless, at 9.00pm on the day of the crime, Gamble was taken into custody, on suspicion of being involved in the murder of Sidney Dowling.

It soon became clear that if Gamble were responsible for the death of Sidney Dowling, then a possible motive, was revenge. When Ellen Dowling was informed of the arrest, she told the police that she had had a problem with Gamble some months before. A stray dog had run into her house and Gamble, who was in the street at the time, had run into her house to try to chase it out. The dog ran all over the house, chased all the time by Gamble, and at one stage ran into Ellen's bedroom. Only when both the dog and Gamble had left, did she miss a valuable watch, which had been in the bedroom. She made an official complaint against Gamble, but the police advised her to drop the matter, as there was not enough evidence against him. Could Gamble have killed the child in order to revenge himself upon Ellen Dowling?

The inquest on the dead child took place on Friday, 9 October, and the evidence against Gamble was soon seen to be contradictory. Whilst it was true that he was the only person known to have access to the house, where the crime took place, anyone else might have entered whilst he was unloading the cart, as he had, of necessity, left the premises unlocked. He had given Sidney the pear, but Jessie Murphy had seen him eating that, whilst sitting on the front step. That meant that Gamble would have had to entice the child into number 41, after he had given him the piece of fruit. Finally, there was the fact that although the crime was committed in a space of perhaps fifteen minutes, Gamble was not late back to the stall in Chapel Street. The coroner advised the jury that it was unsafe to return a verdict against Gamble, and they duly decided that Sidney Dowling had been murdered by a person or persons unknown. Alfred Gamble was a free man, but his story did not end there.

There were two further incidents linked directly to this case. In the first of these, in December 1895, a man confessed to Sidney's murder.

George Clifton had been in prison since his arrest on 5 November, on a charge of stealing a book valued at two shillings. Whilst in prison, he made a full confession to the child's murder saying: 'It was me that killed the child Victor [sic] Dowling, at Parkfield Street. I put the paper in his mouth, then tied him in a sack and threw it over the wall. I heard it sound on the dustbin.

'The reason I make this confession, is because the child is all the while haunting me, and the last three or four nights I have not been able to get any sleep at all.'

What might have looked to be a closure of the case, proved to be nothing of the kind, when the police discovered that Clifton had only recently been released from the Richmond Lunatic Asylum in Dublin, and knew none of the details of the crime, apart from what he had read in the newspaper. He was, nevertheless, given three months' hard labour for stealing the book.

The second development took place on 3 December 1895, when a three-year-old boy, William Charles Cattle, was enticed from his home, at 20 Sidney Grove, into a stable yard next to his house, at number 18. The boy was not discovered until after 7.00pm that evening. He had been suffocated and stabbed but, fortunately, later made a full recovery from his injuries.

The police investigation showed that the stables, at number 18, belonged to none other that Mrs Burgess, the owner of the fruit stall in Chapel Street. She told the police that she had sent an assistant to the stables to get some sacks for her. The assistant was the only person with the key at the time William Cattle had been attacked, and had been an inordinately long time on his errand. That assistant was Alfred Gamble.

Arrested again and charged with wounding and attempted murder, Gamble appeared at the Old Bailey on 13 January 1896, before Mr Justice Hawkins. There were only two witnesses, both medical gentlemen.

Dr George Edward Walker was the surgeon at Holloway prison, where Gamble had been held. The other witness was Dr George Henry Savage, of Henrietta Street. Both doctors had examined Gamble and testified that he was a congenital imbecile and, therefore, not in a fit condition to plead, or understand the nature and quality of the act he had committed. At the direction of the judge, the jury returned a verdict that Alfred Gamble was guilty but insane. He was then ordered to be detained until Her Majesty's pleasure be made known.

Technically, the murder of Sidney Victor Dowling remains an unsolved crime, but what is certain is that after Gamble had been sent down on 13 January, no further investigation into the murder took place.

# Chapter 24

# Alfred Chipperfield
## 1895

When she was just two years old, Maria Clarke had been adopted by George and Ann Brandon, who lived in Leighton Buzzard. Maria grew up in a loving and secure home until, when she was seventeen, in December 1893, she left home and moved to London.

In the capital, Maria earned her living as a barmaid. Her first position was in the *Ram and Teazle* but, by late 1895, she was working at *The Star*. It was in the first of those establishments that she met a young man named Alfred Chipperfield, though he later became a regular customer at *The Star* too. In both establishments, Chipperfield usually came in with a good friend of his, Frank Cannon.

In due course, Maria started walking out with Chipperfield, and they seemed to be very happy in each other's company. Maria often visited her adoptive parents, back in Leighton Buzzard and, some time in November 1895, she took Chipperfield with her, for the first time. There was, however, one small problem. Throughout all this time, Ann Brandon had made it plain that she simply did not approve of the relationship between her adopted daughter and Chipperfield. This wasn't because she had anything in particular against Chipperfield, but simply because she felt Maria was far too young to be romantically involved with any man.

On 13 November, Maria spent an extended stay with her family back in Leighton Buzzard. She stayed until 7 December, but was back again ten days later, on 17 December. This time, Chipperfield was with her, and Maria announced that they had eloped to Cork in Ireland and had married there. From now on, she was to be known as Maria Chipperfield. The newlyweds stayed with the Brandons that night and, next day, caught the train back to London.

John Stanley was a cab driver, and on the evening of Wednesday 18 December 1895, his hansom was parked on the forecourt at Euston railway station. At 9.15pm, a train arrived, and a young couple approached his cab. The couple were Alfred and Maria Chipperfield and, as they climbed in to Stanley's cab, Alfred said that they wished to be taken to Annette Crescent, which was off Essex Road in Islington.

Almost as soon as the journey started, Alfred called for the driver to stop. He had seen that the refreshment bar was open. John Stanley waited patiently, whilst his fares both enjoyed a quick glass of ale together. The journey finally started but, once again, Alfred called for Stanley to stop, as they reached the *White Horse* on Liverpool Road. Alfred went into the bar and returned with a glass of wine, which he gave to his wife. He then invited the cab driver to join him in the bar, for a glass. Stanley agreed, after all, the customer was always right and, if he were prepared to pay, then who was he to argue?

The two men went into the *White Horse*, leaving Maria in the cab with her glass of wine. When the men came out, Alfred announced that he was just going away for a short time, and asked Stanley to wait for him. In fact, Alfred was gone for almost an hour, during which time Maria complained that she was cold. Stanley went back inside the *White Horse,* and brought out a glass of port and a sandwich for his passenger. They then sat and waited for Alfred to return.

Alfred finally arrived back at the cab, and asked Stanley to drive off. The cab moved along the road and had reached Essex Road, just a few yards from Annette Crescent, when Thomas Brown, a man who had been walking down Essex Road, ran to the cab and ordered the driver to stop, saying that there was something terribly wrong.

John Stanley stopped the cab and, looking down, saw that Maria's head was hanging out of the cab window, with her hand grasping for the door handle. Stanley jumped down from his cab and helped Thomas Brown to open the cab door. Only now could both men see that there was a good deal of blood around Maria's throat. As she staggered out of the cab, she tried to say something and pointed towards her throat. As Stanley and some others, who had by now rushed to help, carried Maria to the doctor's, Thomas Brown looked inside the cab. He saw Alfred Chipperfield slumped in the far corner of the cab, apparently unconscious, and bleeding from a wound in his own throat. Brown ran off to find a policeman. He did not have to go very far.

Constable William Capper was on point duty in Essex Road, when Brown approached him, and said that two people had had their throats cut in a cab. Going to investigate, Capper saw Alfred. Still slumped down in the cab. With assistance, the stricken man was taken out, and escorted to Dr Robinson's surgery. By the time Alfred arrived there, Maria had already died.

Alfred Chipperfield was eventually taken to St Bartholomew's Hospital, where he remained until 3 January 1896. On that day he was discharged, but immediately arrested on two charges: one of murder and one of attempting to take his own life. He appeared at the Old Bailey, to answer those charges, on 3 February 1896.

Ann Brandon was the first witness. She started by saying that she had been taken to Holloway mortuary on 19 December, and had there identified the body of Maria Chipperfield, who had previously been named Clarke.

Ann Stroud lived in Westminster, and she confirmed that the dead woman had been her niece. On 6 December, the day before Maria had left Leighton Buzzard to return to London, Ann had received a letter from her. This read:

My dear Uncle and Aunt.
Just a line to say I am coming up to London. Alf wants me to be married in London. I have asked him to put it off till Sunday, as I want a few things. Mother is so nasty; she won't advise me; indeed, if she knew where, she would stop it. We are going to Ireland, if we are married, for ten days, etc., your loving niece, Maria.

Ann was also able to confirm that another letter, found amongst Alfred Chipperfield's belongings, was also in Maria's hand. This one read:

> My dear Alf,
> Just a line to say I will be at Euston, as arranged, tomorrow Friday. I shall come by the 11.20 from Leighton.
>
> Alf, dear, I think it best to wait until Sunday before we are married, as there are one or two things I should like to get, for instance, a coloured dress. If I am ever married at all, it shall not be in a black dress, as you know time is so short that I cannot get one here.
>
> If you had told me a week or two ago, I could have had everything ready, so I hope you will consider this as best, and postpone it for two days, it will not make much difference, will it? Mother is very nasty about it; I shall be glad to get away from here again. I hope you got home all right last night, as I did. I don't think I have any more to say until I see you to-morrow, so will conclude with fondest love.

Herbert Austin confirmed that Alfred had worked for his company since early 1891, but his employment had ceased on Thursday 6 December 1895. On that day, Alfred had asked permission to go into the City, on some private business of his own. Herbert had agreed and said that, as he was going anyway, Alfred could pay some cheques into the company account for him. He could also cash a £15 cheque to cover staff wages. By 3.15pm, Alfred had not returned and, upon checking at the bank, Herbert discovered that Alfred had cashed the cheque and, presumably, absconded with the funds.

At this point, other letters were read out in court. The first of these had been written to Annie, by Alfred, and was dated 22 June 1895. It read:

> To Miss Clark,
> Dear Annie, If you only knew how I feel, you would be sorry for writing to me like this. I love you from the bottom of my heart, and no one else shall have you. I am not going in the

Ram any more, and don't tell people all you know, because it only comes back. Trusting you are quite well, with love.

The second letter was dated just over a month later, on 29 July. It began:

Dear Annie, You greatly upset me last night.

I thought when I came in on Sunday morning there was something wrong, with my not wanting to take you out in the afternoon. I should only have been too pleased to do so, but as it was such a wretched day, and being a Sunday, I did not think you would care to come.

I have turned over a new leaf, and feel much better for it. I want you to meet me at the Bank tomorrow. I have something I wish to ask you. It is not very nice for me to come and see you, when you are making arrangements with other fellows. Anybody would think I was a fool.

I had no sleep all last night through you. I think it is very unkind of you to go on like this, when I am trying to do my best for you. I have been greatly upset lately without you making more trouble. I was going abroad, only I put it off for you.

You know I love you, and would do anything for you. Of course, if you do not like me, I would rather you tell me, than to make a fool of me. I can assure you that since we made it up, I have not been with one girl. I shall not say any more at present, so trusting you are quite well.

Those letters indicated that all had not, after all, been well with the relationship between the two lovers. Both had apparently been jealous of other people and it might well be argued that Alfred was rushing Maria into marriage, in the hope that this would solve whatever problems they had. It also gave a possible motive for Alfred wishing to kill Maria, if he were jealous of other men paying her attention.

After John Stanley, the cab driver and Thomas Brown, who had first seen Maria hanging out of the cab window, had given their evidence, the prosecution called other witnesses to some of the events in Essex Road, on the night Maria was killed.

Alfred Griffiths had been close to Annette Crescent when he heard a woman scream. Seeing the cab stop, and other people running towards it, Griffiths went to see for himself what had taken place. He helped to take Maria to Dr Richardson's but he was not at home. As Maria was helped into the empty surgery, it was Griffiths who ran off to fetch Dr Gray.

William Edward Wright was also near Annette Crescent, and went to offer what assistance he could. Wright was another of the men, who had helped to carry Maria into Dr Richardson's surgery.

Sergeant Hugh Harley was called to Dr Richardson's surgery some time after Maria had died. After Alfred Chipperfield had received basic treatment for the wound in his throat, it was Harley who escorted him to St Bartholomew's Hospital. The prisoner was searched there, and Harley found an empty razor case in one of his jacket pockets.

During his stay in the hospital, Alfred was guarded by police officers. One of those officers was Constable John Ashton. On 19 December, whilst he was at the prisoner's bed, Alfred touched him on the arm and said: 'Have you seen my wife?' When Ashton said that he hadn't, Alfred continued, saying:

> She is in the mortuary. I wish it was me instead of her, for she was a good girl.
>
> We were married on Monday, and came to London on Wednesday. We took a cab from Euston, and stopped just outside the station, and had a drink, and then stopped again at the *White Hart* public house, on Liverpool Road.
>
> I left my wife there some time, and went to try and find a pal of mine, Frank Cannon, but could not find him. I got in the cab again, and we drove down Essex Road.
>
> I remember we were all right when we passed the *Brewers'* public house, but I don't remember anything after that, only drawing the razor across my own throat. I suppose I must have cut her throat; but, my God, I should not like to think I did. We were going to call at my father's house, in Annette Crescent.

The Frank Cannon who Alfred had referred to, was the next witness. He said he lived at 30 White Lion Street, in Clerkenwell, and had known the prisoner for some five years. On the night Maria was killed, Frank was not at home, so could not say why Alfred had wished to see him.

The medical evidence at the trial was to prove highly contentious, and formed the basis of Alfred Chipperfield's defence. The first doctor called to the stand was Dr Malachi Joseph Robinson. He had arrived back at his surgery to find Dr Gray treating Alfred for a wound to his throat. Maria was also there, but she was quite dead by this time. Dr Robinson had been with Dr Gray when the post-mortem was carried out on Maria's body. He reported a wound three and a half inches long, which had divided the carotid artery on the left side, and the windpipe. In Dr Robinson's opinion, the wound was self-inflicted, by a left-handed person.

The second medical witness was Dr Thomas Underwood Gray. After stating that he agreed with Dr Robinson's post-mortem report, he went on to say that he also agreed that Maria's wound was most probably self-inflicted, and again by a left handed person.

The third, and final medical witness, was Dr Thomas Bond, a surgeon at the Westminster Hospital, and a lecturer in forensic medicine. Whilst not actually insulting the previous two witnesses, Dr Bond gently pointed out that whilst they might well be excellent general practitioners, they had not had experience of murder cases before, and were not used to dealing with such crimes of violence. Dr Bond, on the other hand, had years of such experience and had worked with the police on dozens of murder cases. He testified that whilst Alfred's wound was undoubtedly self-inflicted, Maria's was not. There was also the fact that Maria's family had stated that she was right-handed.

The jury only took a few minutes to decide that Alfred had murdered Maria and he was then sentenced to death. Twenty-two days later, on Tuesday 25 February 1896, Alfred Chipperfield was hanged at Newgate, by James Billington and William Warbrick. It was said that he showed no fear, and marched to the gallows like a soldier.

# Chapter 25

# John Grande, Charles Barrett and Alfred Jones

## 1899

At around 4.20pm, on Wednesday 30 August 1899, William Button, a 'carman', was driving his trap down Caledonian Road towards Albion Street, in Islington. It was just as he passed the *Queen's Head* public house that he noticed a group of four men, in conversation, and an elderly gentleman walking down the street towards them.

After the man had passed them, the four men began following him and, since Button was driving at a mere walking pace, it meant that they kept pace with his vehicle. He was able to see clearly as one of the group of four dashed behind his trap, ran up beside it, and then ran in front, so that he was now positioned in front of the old man. He then stopped the man, and the other three piled into him and began to jostle him. Button saw the first man snatch a watch, and then all four men ran off, as the elderly gentleman fell to the ground, his head catching on the pavement.

William Button jumped down from his trap, and went to help the injured man. He was later taken to the Royal Free Hospital, where he was identified as sixty-three-year-old Henry Benbow, the identification being made through items he was carrying on his person.

Henry was attended to by Dr Thomas Percy Legg, the House Surgeon, who first saw his patient at 5.00pm. He was suffering from a large cut, some two inches long, at the back of his head. There was a good deal of dirt in the wound and Dr Legg dressed it carefully, before telling him to wait. When the doctor returned, however, Henry Benbow had left the hospital.

A dazed Henry had returned to his home, but he was still suffering from the effects of his fall. That same evening, his family physician, Dr Thomas Walter Coffin, was called to see him. When the doctor arrived, Henry was in bed. An examination showed that he was suffering from a compound fracture of the skull. Once again, the wound was dressed.

The next day, Thursday 31 August, Dr Coffin called on Henry again. He was now complaining of a severe headache and this was followed, over the next day or so, by fits and convulsions. As part of his treatment, Dr Coffin trepanned the area around the wound, and this did seem to give some relief, but it was only temporary. At 1.40am on 4 September, Henry Benbow died.

William Button, and other witnesses, had given excellent descriptions of the men they had seen attacking Henry Benbow, and the police felt sure that they knew the names of at least three of them.

Detective Constable Walter Selby saw the first of the wanted men on 6 September, at the Barnet Horse Fair. The man, twenty-three-year-old John Grande, was standing outside a booth, when Selby approached him and said he wished to speak to him, in connection with assaulting and robbing a man in Albion Street. At this stage, no mention was made of the fact that Henry had died, so Grande most probably believed that the charge he would face, would be a relatively minor one. He made no attempt to hide his involvement asking only: 'How many have you got?' When Selby informed him that he was the first, Grande replied: 'It is just my luck. I am first again.'

It was Constable Selby who also made the second arrest, later that same day. Acting on information he had received from Grande, Selby went to the *Old King's Head* beer house in Euston Road, where he found Charles Barrett standing outside, enjoying a pint. When told he was to be arrested, Barrett replied: 'I know nothing about it.'

On the same day, 6 September, again acting on information received, Detective Constable George Godley visited an address in Robert Street, where he arrested the third man, Alfred Jones. He also denied knowing anything about the attack upon Henry Benbow.

The trial of the three prisoners took place on 23 October, with each man being charged with robbery and manslaughter. All three pleaded not guilty to both charges.

William Button told the court what he had seen in Albion Street. After Henry Benbow had fallen to the ground, he had gone to his aid, cradling his bleeding head in his lap and placing his handkerchief around the wound. Since that date, he had been to attend three separate identity parades. He had had no trouble in picking out the three men now standing in the dock. On 7 September, he had picked out Grande and Barrett and at a later date, 6 October, he had picked out Jones.

George Frederick Barnes had been passing down Albion Street, when he saw four men abusing an old man, who he now knew to be Henry Benbow. As Henry fell, the four men ran directly past Barnes, who got a good look at all of them. Barnes too had picked out all three men at identity parades.

Thirteen-year-old Ellen Hagan was coming home from school on 30 August, when she saw three men running from the direction of the *Queen's Head*. She testified that Barrett was the one who had hit Mr Benbow before he fell. Ellen had identified two of the men since: Barrett and Jones.

Charles Jared, who was also aged thirteen, was another of the people in Albion Street at the time that Henry Benbow was attacked. The men had run quite close to him as they made their escape, and Jared had later picked out two that he knew from the district: Barrett and Jones.

Asked if they had anything to say in their own defence, Barrett said that he was at Waterloo Station at the time of the attack. Grande merely replied: 'I am innocent.' Jones claimed that he had lived in the area for about twenty years, which is how people knew him. He then tried to discredit one of the witnesses, Charles Jared, by saying that he knew the family well, and they were all brothel keepers.

All three were found guilty of manslaughter and only now could it be revealed that Grande had four previous convictions for violent theft, whilst Jones had nine. All three were then given terms of imprisonment. John Grande and Alfred Jones were both given ten years whilst Charles Barrett, as this was his first known offence, received just five, even though the evidence had indicated that he was the man who had struck Benbow. The fourth man who had been involved in the attack, was never traced.

# Chapter 26

# Other Crimes
# 1851-1900

### (1) Peter Leggatt, 1853

On Monday 3 October 1853, a gang of men was working on the new market in Copenhagen Fields. A rather elderly gentleman was in charge of the gang and, as a load of rubble arrived, to be used for filling, a man approached, and asked if he could have some.

The ganger said that he wasn't able to give out any of the rubble, whereupon the man, Peter Leggatt, suggested that they should fight. Then as if to emphasis the seriousness of this request, Leggatt lashed out and struck the ganger in the eye.

It was at this point that one of the workmen, George Drew, marched forward and told the stranger that he was a coward, for challenging such an old man and, if he really wanted to fight, then he would be more than happy to accommodate him.

The other workmen formed a ring as Leggatt and Drew began to fight. It was decided that each knock-down would signal the end of a round and both man fell at various times, during the fight, though Drew seemed to be getting much the best of his opponent. It was not until the seventh round, that Leggatt finally landed a severe blow, striking Drew beneath his ear. Drew staggered, then pulled himself up onto one knee, before falling back again. His workmates picked him up, and carried him to the *City of London Tavern*.

Fortuitously, one of the men passing by this scene happened to be a doctor. Dr Thomas Murphy saw the group of men, towards the end of the fight, and observed one of the protagonists being carried into a nearby tavern. Dr Murphy followed, to see if he could offer any professional help, but, upon arrival in the public house, discovered that he was too late. George Drew was already dead.

The post-mortem was carried out by Dr Edward Cousins, who stated that the cause of death was certainly the blow beneath the ear. This had, in turn, caused acute pressure on the brain, at the top of the spinal column.

Charged with manslaughter, Leggatt appeared before Mr Justice Williams, at the Old Bailey, on 24 October. Found guilty, he was, nevertheless, strongly recommended to mercy. Witnesses to the fight had stated, that in each round, Drew had grabbed Leggatt by the hair, and punched him, and it was not really until the end of the fight, that Leggatt had even struck a blow. That recommendation was given weight and, consequently, Leggatt received just one month's imprisonment.

## (2) James Saywood, 1864

James Saywood managed to commit his crime in front of, arguably, one of the best witnesses available, a policeman.

On 19 September 1864, Constable William Pearce was in Elder Walk, when he saw two men, Saywood and Michael Dunn, exchanging heated words. Even as Pearce walked towards the two men, to see what the problem was, Saywood struck Dunn in the chest, knocking him to the ground. He then kicked out, striking Dunn in the head. He was immediately taken into custody.

In fact, Constable Pearce was in the vicinity because of an earlier problem, at Dunn's house. Eliza Sticks, a woman, who lived with Saywood as his wife, had been accused of assaulting Dunn's sister, Margaret. Pearce and another constable, had gone to Saywood's home, to arrest his lover, and it was as Eliza was pulling her boots on to go with the officers, that Saywood had shouted that he would go out and give that bastard Dunn his bloody oats. Pearce had followed Saywood outside, leaving his brother officer to take the Eliza into custody.

That brother officer was Constable George Taylor. Once the attack upon Michael Dunn had taken place, Pearce called him outside to assist. By the time Taylor arrived, Dunn was lying unconscious on the ground. Saywood, meanwhile, had been arrested, without a struggle.

Michael Dunn was taken to the infirmary, at the Islington workhouse, and it was there that he was seen by Dr Joseph Ricksby Donald. He saw a deep, contused wound on the top of Dunn's head. The injured man was kept in the infirmary for treatment, but died on 15 October, making this now a case of manslaughter. However, when Dr Donald did the post-mortem, he ascribed the death of Dunn to a disease of the lungs. The wound to his head had, in Dr Donald's opinion, caused a fever, which had worsened the condition of Dunn's lungs. In short, if he had not been injured in the fight, Dunn would, in all probability, have recovered from the fever that killed him.

James Saywood appeared at the Old Bailey on 24 October 1864. The prosecution only called the two policemen sent to the house, and Dr Donald, before the defence called their own witnesses.

Sarah Cunningham said that she had heard the original argument between Saywood and Dunn, out in Elder Walk. It was Dunn's brother, Frederick, who first stripped off his shirt, ready to fight. Moments later, it was Michael Dunn who started the fight. Finally, Saywood was very drunk at the time, and did not seem to know what he was doing.

Henry Wilkinson lived in Elder Walk, and he told the court that he had heard Michael Dunn using the foulest language, before the altercation started. Henry also said that he had known Saywood for twenty years or more, and had always considered him to be a quiet chap.

Despite this testimony, James Saywood was found guilty of manslaughter. However, it appeared that the trial judge felt that this crime was not entirely Saywood's fault, for he sentenced him to serve just four months in prison.

### (3) Savena Tompkins, 1869

In June, 1869, Susannah Nevill, a servant-girl living in Alma Street, Hoxton, gave birth to a baby, a heathly boy, whom she named James. The father of the child was Mr Wallace, Susannah's master, and he agreed to pay for the upkeep of the boy. However, the child could not remain in his house, so had to be sent out, for a nurse to take care of. A suitable woman was found in Mrs Davis, of 14 Dean Street, also in Hoxton, and a sum of seven shilling per week was agreed.

At around 8.30pm, on Monday 5 July, Mrs Davis told one of the other lodgers at her house, Savena Tompkins, that she had to go out for an hour or so, and asked Savena if she would keep an ear open in case the baby cried. Savena was happy to oblige.

Mrs Davis did not return home until 10.00pm and, going to check on the baby, found that he was not in his cot. There was also no sign of Savena. The alarm was raised but, by this time, James Nevill had already been found. His dead body had been discovered, wrapped in a bundle, in Canonbury Place, Islington. As for Savena Tompkins, when she returned home, she was arrested on a charge of murdering the child.

The inquest opened at the *Old Parr's Head Tavern*, in Upper Street, on Thursday 8 July. By this time, medical evidence had shown that James had died, as a result of suffocation, but the doctor was unable to say if this had been deliberate. It was equally likely that he might have suffocated in his cot, a condition we now refer to as cot death syndrome.

An important witness was Elizabeth Westerham. Not only was she Mrs Davis sister, but she also employed Savena Tompkins. This meant that her testimony was crucial for both women.

Elizabeth testified that on the night in question, Savena had called at her home at around 9.00pm, with some linen. At 10.00pm, her sister, Mrs Davis called and asked if Savena had had the baby with her, as it was now missing. Half an hour later, Savena was back saying that she had returned home, and found James gone.

The coroner said that he found this to be a most curious case. He could think of no person, who had a motive to deliberately kill James Nevill. Mrs Davis had an interest in keeping the child alive, as she was being paid for his upkeep. Savena had nothing to do with the child, and had no reason for wishing him dead. A more likely scenario was that the child had died naturally, been found by someone, and then dumped in Islington out of fear. The question was, who had dumped the body?

The police had, by now, come to believe that Savena had played no part in this. They now suggested that Mrs Davis had found James dead, had asked Savena to look out for him, dumped the body in Islington, and then visited her sister to implicate Savena in his death. At this, Elizabeth Westerham shouted that it was wicked to accuse her sister of killing the child. The coroner replied that he had made no such accusation.

The jury had to decide if the child was murdered and if so, who had committed the crime. In the event, they returned the verdict that James had died from suffocation but, how it occurred, and who had then conveyed the child's body to Islington, there was not sufficient evidence to show. Savena Tompkins, almost certainly innocent of any involvement, was then released from custody.

## (4) Charles Morgan, 1883

On the afternoon of Saturday 1 September 1883, Charles Morgan was in the Favourite beer house, playing dominoes with William Cummings, and two other men named George Butterfield and a Mr Harris. Money was changing hands, on the outcome of the various games, and everyone appeared to be friendly enough.

At one stage, Cummings wife called him out of the tavern, as she wished to speak to him. Cummings left the game, and asked Morgan to play his hand for him. That hand carried a side bet, of a round of drinks.

When Cummings returned he found that Morgan had lost the hand, meaning that he had to pay 4d for the round. Angry at this, he insisted that Morgan should pay it for him, as it had been who had lost the hand. Morgan refused, and after arguing about the matter for some time, the two men went outside to fight.

It was Morgan who was getting the better of the match, and at one stage, just as Cummings was falling, Morgan lashed out and caught him with another punch. The force of that blow increased the speed with which Cummings fell and caused his head to be dashed against the kerbstone, killing him instantly.

Charged with manslaughter, Morgan appeared at the Old Bailey on 15 October, and after hearing the evidence, Morgan's defence barrister, Mr Thorne Cole, told the judge, that he could offer no argument against the prisoner being responsible for the death of William Cummings.

Found guilty, Morgan received the extremely lenient sentence of just three days' imprisonment.

### (5) George Henry Swiney, 1886

At some time after 9.30pm, on 7 June 1886, Susannah Coliver was walking along Englefield Road, pushing her sixteen-month-old baby, in a perambulator, in front of her. Then, just as she was about to push the pram across the road, a dray cart turned into the street, from Essex Road, travelling at a very high speed.

So furiously was the cart being driven, that Susannah had to pull her pram back from the edge of the kerb. The dray missed her baby by mere inches, but an old gentleman, just a few steps away from Susannah, was struck by the wheels and the shafts, and was dashed down into the road, where the dray ran over his body.

Sarah called out for the cart to stop, but the driver either didn't hear, or simply choose to ignore her, for her carried on down the street, hardly slowing at all, until Abraham Cohen, who was further along the street, dashed out into the road and stopped him.

The dray driver, George Swiney, was escorted back to the scene of the accident, and various witnesses saw that he was very drunk. The police and a doctor were called and, when the elderly victim, Thomas Drover, was found to be dead, Swiney was taken into custody, and charged with manslaughter.

Swiney's trial took place on 28 June, three weeks to the day after Drover had been killed. Simeon Lang had been behind the dray as it turned, at speed into Englefield Road, and saw it run over Thomas Drover. The wheels passed directly over Drover's chest.

Emily Goodhart was in Essex Road, so did not see the accident itself, but she did see a number of people gathered around Swiney and the injured man, as she passed into Englefield Road. She believed that Swiney was very drunk, and unsteady on his feet.

Constable James Ranyard arrived at the scene of the tragedy, a little before 10.00pm. He arrested Swiney, and escorted him to the police station, where he was charged with manslaughter.

Dr Thomas Underwood Bray had his surgery at 240 Essex Road, and he was called to the scene. The location was very dark indeed, and the doctor had to make his examination by the light of matches, struck by one of the bystanders. Drover was already dead, and Dr Bray performed the post-mortem on 10 June. He found a ruptured heart and spleen, eight broken ribs on the left side, a broken sternum and a broken breast bone.

Two witnesses were called to testify to Swiney's character. Thomas Ball said that he had known the prisoner for almost fourteen years, and knew him as a most careful and considerate driver. Ball was, however, unable to comment as to Swiney's fondness, or otherwise, for alcohol.

The final witness was Charles William Ewin, the landlord of the *Vicar of Wakefield* public house, in Bethnal Green. He testified that Swiney had driven him, and his family for three years. He had also been a customer of Ewin's pub, but he had never seen him drunk.

The jury, however, gave more credence to the witnesses at the scene and found Swiney guilty of manslaughter, though they did recommend him to mercy, on account of his previous good character. The trial judge then sentenced Swiney to eighteen months in prison, with hard labour.

# Chapter 27

# George Chapman
## 1903

At 12.30pm, on Wednesday 22 October 1902, Maud Eliza Marsh died at the *Crown* public house at High Street, Islington. The medical gentleman who had attended to Maud refused to issue a death certificate. The reason for this was that in 1901, Dr James Maurice Stoker had also been the physician to another lady, who had died at a public house. Both women displayed identical symptoms, and the same man had been the paramour of the deceased. The doctor was convinced that he had witnessed one, possibly two cases of poisoning, and determined that a post-mortem was necessary.

That examination was carried out the following day, 23 October, and no disease that would have caused Maud's death was found. That made the circumstances look even more like a case of poisoning, but Dr Stoker's tests for arsenic also proved to be negative. If, indeed, a poison had been used, it was not one of the more common ones. Dr Stoker took some tissue and organ samples from the dead woman, carefully sealed them in clean containers, and passed them on to Dr Richard Bodmer of the Clinical Research Association.

To double check, Dr Bodmer also began by testing for arsenic and found only normal, minimal traces of that substance. The tests involved slips of copper and Dr Bodmer noted that they had changed to a purple colour, suggesting the presence of antimony. Another test was tried and this confirmed that antimony was present, in much greater quantities than the arsenic. Dr Bodmer surmised that Maud Marsh had died as a result of being poisoned with tartar emetic, an antimony based poison, which usually contained small amounts of arsenic, as an impurity. Three days after Maud's death, on Saturday 25

October, the man who had been living with Maud, as her husband, George Chapman, was arrested and charged with her murder, under his real name of Severin Antoniovitch Klosowski.

When the police investigated Klosowski's antecedents they found that he had certainly led a chequered life. Born in Poland on 14 December 1865, he had left school when he was fourteen, and been apprenticed to a surgeon for four and a half years. In October 1885 he had moved to Warsaw, where he was employed as an assistant surgeon until November 1886.

By 1888, he was living in London, and working in a barber's shop below the White Hart, at 89 Whitechapel High Street. In August 1889 he had married a woman named Lucy Baderski, and she had given birth to a son soon afterwards. The family moved to the United States in May 1890, where their young son died.

By 1891, the couple were back in London, where, on 12 May, Lucy gave birth to their second child, a daughter. The relationship was, however, already in trouble, mainly due to Klosowski's fondness for other women and, in April 1893, Lucy left her husband.

By 1895, Klosowski was living with a woman named Annie Chapman, and although that relationship also did not last for very long, Klosowski started using her surname, and from that time onwards, called himself George Chapman. That same year, Chapman became an assistant hairdresser at the shop of William Wenzel, at 7 Church Lane, Leytonstone. One of his customers, John Ward, offered Chapman a furnished room, and it was in his house that Chapman met a widow, Mary Isabella Spink, a woman who preferred to use her second name.

Chapman soon started a relationship with Isabella and the couple, now living as man and wife, moved to Hastings in 1896, where he set up a hairdresser's, at 10 Hill Street. By February 1897, the couple had returned to London, and Chapman had decided on a new trade. He took on the licence of the *Prince of Wales* public house, in Bartholomew Street, off Old Street, Finsbury. It was there, on 25 December, that same year, that Isabella died after a short illness.

In 1898, Chapman had advertised for a new barmaid, and the woman who obtained the position, was Elizabeth Taylor, known to her friends as Bessie. Chapman was soon involved in a relationship with Bessie, and there was much gossip about the improper behaviour at the *Prince of Wales*. That was why Chapman took a new lease, on *The Grapes*, at Bishop's Stortford, but the couple returned to London the following year.

On 23 March 1899, Chapman and Bessie took a lease on the *Monument* in Union Street, Islington. Less than two years later, on 13 February 1901, Bessie died. She too had suffered a short illness, and the attending doctor had been Dr James Maurice Stoker, the same gentleman who had grown suspicious when a second woman, Maud Marsh had died, in a similar manner.

The more the police discovered, the more certain they were that there now might, possibly, be three cases of murder to consider. Tests had already shown that Maud Marsh had been poisoned with tartar emetic, and Chapman was in custody on a charge of murdering her. Two other women, Isabella Spink and Bessie Taylor, had died in very similar circumstances and so, might also have been poisoned. The police decided that both bodies would have to be exhumed.

On 22 November 1902, Bessie Taylor's body was exhumed. Some two weeks later, on 9 December, Isabella's body was also exhumed. Both bodies were found to be remarkably well preserved, and the subsequent examinations of their remains, led to the conclusion that both had indeed been poisoned with antimony. On 31 December 1902, Chapman was charged with two more murders.

The trial of George Chapman opened on 18 March 1903, before Mr Justice Grantham. During the four days the proceedings lasted, Chapman was defended by Mr George Elliott, Mr Arthur Hutton and Mr V Lyons. The case for the Crown was led by the Solicitor General, Mr Sutton, who was assisted by Mr Charles Mathews and Mr Bodkin.

At the very start, Mr Elliott, for the defence, asked the judge to rule that only evidence relating to the offence Chapman was being tried for, the murder of Maud Marsh, should be heard, and the prosecution should make no reference to the other two charges, as they were separate indictments. After considering the opposing legal arguments, Mr Justice Grantham ruled that evidence on all three cases could be used.

The first witness was Wolff Levisohn, a traveller in hairdresser's appliances. He testified that he had known Chapman since 1888, but at the time, Chapman was using the name Ludwig Zagovski. The two men encountered each other, in the course of their business, on a fairly regular basis until 1890. Both men had served as faldschers, or doctor's assistants, and it was natural that they sometimes talked about medicine. At one stage, around about 1890, Chapman had asked Wolff if he could get him some tartar emetic. Wolff had refused to co-operate, saying that he did not wish to get twelve years in jail.

Stanislaus Baderski was a tailor living in Walthamstow, and he had known Chapman for some thirteen years. Stanislaus told the court that he had two sisters, one of whom was named Lucy. Chapman had met Lucy at the Polish Club in St John's Square, Clerkenwell, and after walking out together for just a few weeks, they got married, on the August Bank Holiday in 1889. The relationship lasted until April 1893, when Lucy left him due to his womanising ways.

Detective Inspector George Godley told the court that he had arrested Chapman, at the *Crown* in Islington. Afterwards, Godley had searched the premises and taken away a number of documents, written in Polish. These documents had been handed to a translator.

That translator was the next witness, Joseph Betrikowski. The first document was a copy of Chapman's birth certificate, which showed that, on 14 December 1865, Antonio Klosowski, a carpenter, and his wife, Emilie had had a son whom they had named Severin. Another document, a reference of some sort, dated 16 November 1882, stated that Severin Klosowski, a resident of the village of Zvolen, was a well-behaved man, and had never been found guilty of any crime. Other documents referred to Klosowski's medical training, and all stated that he had carried out his duties with zeal and accomplishment.

William Henry Davidson was a retired chemist, now living at 49 Upper Lewes Road, Brighton, but in 1897 he traded from a shop at 66 High Street, Hastings. Davidson had run the Hastings shop for eighteen years and during his time there, had frequented a certain barber's shop for his haircuts and shaves. That shop was run by Klosowski who, at the time, was living with a woman calling herself Isabella Chapman, who was, of course, Mary Isabella Spink.

As part of the legal requirements, Davidson kept a poisons register and this was now produced in court. One entry, dated 3 April 1897, showed that a man signing his name G Chapman, had purchased one ounce of tartar emetic, for which he paid two pence. This was the only sale of tartar emetic within the entire volume.

Davidson had also sold, to the same man, two medical books. He also pointed out that when he had handed the poison over to Chapman, he had marked it with a red label reading poison. Inspector Godley was now recalled to state, that when he had searched the *Crown*, after Chapman's arrest, he had found the two medical books Mr Davidson had referred to. Inside one of the books, was a red label which read 'Poison'.

The next few witnesses gave testimony relating directly to the death of Maud Eliza Marsh. The first of these was Eliza Marsh, the dead woman's mother.

Eliza began by stating that Maud had been born on 17 February 1882. In the early part of the century she had been employed as a barmaid, in Croydon, but lost her position in August 1901. Maud placed an advertisement for a new position and Chapman had replied to it, from the *Monument* public house. An interview was arranged, and Maud had been successful in obtaining the position, which included accommodation.

In the middle of September 1901, Maud and Chapman went to visit Eliza at her home in Croydon, and he said that they were very fond of each other and wished to marry. As a proof of his wish to provide adequately for Maud, Chapman showed Eliza a will, in which he had written that in the event of his death, all his property was to pass to Maud.

On 13 October, Eliza visited Chapman at the *Monument*. She saw that there was a good deal of confetti scattered about. She was then informed, that the couple had married that morning but, curiously, when she asked to look at the marriage certificate, she was told that it was now locked away with Chapman's other papers.

Towards the end of that same year, there was a mysterious fire at the *Monument*, and the insurance company refused to pay out. This did not seem to bother Chapman, who simply took the lease on the *Crown* public house. He and Maud moved there just before Christmas.

For some time, Eliza did not see her daughter until, in July 1902, she received a letter from her, saying that she had been ill, and was now in Guy's Hospital. Eliza visited Maud there a number of times, and was pleased when she made a full recovery, from whatever had been bothering her, and returned to the *Crown*, and Chapman. In October, Maud wrote again to say that she was ill, and Eliza visited her at the *Crown* on 20 October.

When Eliza saw Maud, on the 20th, she complained of pains in the lower part of her stomach, and excessive thirst. Chapman seemed to be ministering well to Maud, and kept giving her drinks of either iced-water or water and brandy. After each such drink, Maud would vomit violently, and Eliza noticed that the vomit had a greenish tinge to it.

Eliza then stated that whilst she was at the house, she took a drink of brandy herself, and added some of the iced water to it. An hour or so later she felt sick and had pains in her stomach. Later she had diarrhoea, and vomited a number of times. Finally, Eliza was able to confirm that Maud had died on 22 October.

Robert Marsh was Eliza's husband and Maud's father, and he had also visited the *Crown* in the days before his daughter died. Robert had also given Maud some of the water which seemed to make her sick immediately after taking it, and noticed that the liquid seemed to be a little discoloured.

On 21 October, at Robert's request, their family doctor, Dr Francis Gaspard Grapel, had called to see Maud, and when Robert saw her later that same day, she appeared to be slightly better. Seeing Chapman downstairs in the bar later, Robert had remarked: 'I think my daughter will pull through now, George.' Chapman had replied: 'She will never get up no more.'

Louisa Sarah Morris was the married sister of Maud Marsh. She was in the habit of visiting Maud at the *Monument*, and recalled her being admitted to Guy's Hospital in July and August 1902. Louisa recalled a conversation she had had with Chapman, when they had moved to the *Crown*. Maud was back in hospital, and had asked her sister to bring some personal things for her, from the pub. Whilst she was at the *Crown*, Louisa voiced her puzzlement to Chapman, over the illness, which seemed to be recurring. Chapman said: 'She should have done as I had told her.' Whem Louisa asked him what he meant, he replied: 'She should have took [sic] the medicine I told her.'

Later in that same conversation, Louisa said that it was strange that the doctors could not find out what it was that had made Maud so ill. Chapman smiled and replied: 'I could give her a bit like that,' snapping his fingers, 'and fifty doctors would not find out.'

During her final illness, Louisa had spent a good deal of time with Maud. On Saturday 11 October, Louisa went to stay at the *Monument*, and made some Bovril for her sister. That seemed to make her feel better, and she was not sick after taking it. Half an hour later, when Maud said she was thirsty, Louisa gave her some ginger beer that Chapman had sent up from the bar. As soon as she had drunk some of it, Maud was violently sick.

Alice May Marsh was another of Maud's sisters. She had visited Maud at the *Crown* when she first became ill. As she went into the bar, she saw Chapman and asked where Maud was. He replied: 'In bed, dying fast.' It was Alice who took her sister to Guy's Hospital. Chapman did not seem very pleased with this, and complained that the doctors would only 'mess her about.'

Jessie Toon was a regular at the *Crown*, and when Maud fell ill, Chapman asked Jessie if she would nurse her for him. Jessie agreed, and started ministering to Maud on 16 October. During the time she was there, Maud complained constantly of thirst. Various drinks were provided for her, but all were brought up from the bar by Chapman himself.

On 22 October, the day that Maud died, she had asked Jessie for another drink. Chapman brought up some brandy from the bar and added a good deal of water to it, from a jug in the hallway. When this was given to Maud she complained that it burned, so Jessie gave her some water but that seemed to make her sick. Jesie thought that the original brandy might have been too strong a measure for Maud so took a sip herself, to test it. The liquid burned her throat and left a foul taste. So bad was it, that Jessie had to go to the kitchen, and eat some bread and butter to take the taste away.

Louisa Beatrice Cole was a servant at the *Crown*, and she did all of the cooking in the establishment. Louisa recalled one day, in early October, when she had prepared some potatoes and meat for lunch. She and Chapman ate together, but he put some of the potatoes aside for Maud to have later. When Maud did eat them, she was very sick afterwards.

Dr James Henry Targett was a surgeon at Guy's Hospital. He recalled Maud being admitted on 28 July 1902. She remained as a patient until 20 August. When she was admitted she complained of terrible pains in her lower stomach. These were so bad that she could not even bear to be touched during the initial examination. Dr Targett treated her, but she grew worse for the first couple of weeks. It was not until 10 August, that her condition began to improve, and her temperature fell. She was in perfectly good health, at the time she was discharged.

A possible motive, for Maud being poisoned was supplied by Florence Rayner. In June 1902, Florence was employed as a barmaid at the *Crown*, and after only being there for two weeks, Chapman grabbed her, kissed her passionately, and asked her to be his sweetheart, and go to America with him. Florence pointed out to Chapman that he had a wife downstairs.

Chapman, in reply, snapped his fingers and said: 'If I gave her that she would be no more Mrs. Chapman.' Soon after this, Maud had fallen ill, and Florence had left the *Crown* for a new position at the *Foresters*, in Twickenham.

Annie Chapman gave the court information, which showed what kind of a man Chapman really was. She confirmed that they had lived together as man and wife from November 1893, until around December 1894. Soon after she had left him, she had discovered that she was pregnant with his child. Chapman had told her that he was not interested.

Dr Grapel testified that, at Robert Marsh's request, he had visited Maud, at the *Crown* on 21 October. Chapman was most displeased that another doctor had been sent, but Dr Grapel insisted on seeing the patient. Dr Stoker was there, and together the two examined Maud. Her skin was sallow, jaundiced, and muddy in appearance, her tongue was coated, her pulse fairly quick. Her breathing was shallow, and her stomach was extremely tender to the touch. Grapel consulted with Dr Stoker, and they agreed that Maud was suffering from some acute irritant poison, most probably ptomaine. Later, Dr Grapel changed his opinion, and concluded that it might well be arsenic.

Dr James Stoker told the court that Chapman had called at his surgery at 5.00pm on 10 October 1902, and asked for some medicine for his wife, who was suffering from diarrhoea and vomiting. Stoker gave Chapman some medicine and agreed to call on Maud at 10.30pm that evening. He found her complaining of severe stomach pains, and after making his examination, said that she was to have no solid food, but be given soda water and milk, boiled milk, brandy, beef tea and ice, the last item to stop the sickness she was feeling.

By 13 October, there had been no improvement in Maud's condition. By the 15th, she was also suffering from spasms. Bismuth powders were administered, but they seemed to have no effect. Dr Stoker suggested that a nurse should be taken on and, a few days later, found that Chapman had engaged the services of Jessie Toon.

Maud's condition grew steadily worse, and she died at 12.20pm on 22 October. Dr Stoker had been out of his surgery at the time, attending to another patient, and as soon as he received news of Maud's death, he went to the *Crown*. To his surprise, the place was still open for business, and customers were drinking happily in the bar and being served by Chapman. After speaking to him, Dr Stoker said he was not satisfied as to the cause of death and wished a post-mortem to take place. Dr Stoker admitted that the only reason he had suggested the post-mortem, was because the cause of death completely baffled him. He had not, at that time, connected the death with that of Bessie Taylor, but did so very soon afterwards.

After Dr Stoker had performed his post-mortem, and the tests upon the samples removed had indicated antimony poisoning, a second post-mortem had been ordered by the coroner. This had been performed by Dr Thomas Stevenson. He found no natural cause for Maud's death either. He immediately suspected that an irritant poison had been used. His tests confirmed antimony, and showed that a large dose must have been given, within a few hours of death. Having tested the various organs, Dr Stevenson found a total of 7.24 grains of antimony. This, in turn, meant that some 25 to 30 grains of tartar emetic must have been administered. The usual fatal dose was 15 grains.

The prosecution now turned to the other two cases against Chapman. The first witness here was Joseph Smith Renton. He confirmed that he had had a cousin named Mary Isabella Renton, who had married a man named Shadrack Spink. That relationship ended and Renton knew that some time afterwards, Isabella was living with Chapman, as his wife.

John Ward confirmed that he had offered a furnished room to Chapman, and that Isabella Spink was already lodging at his house. One day, not long after Chapman had moved in, Ward's wife complained to him that she had seen Chapman and Isabella kissing on the stairs. Ward told Chapman that he did not approve of such behaviour in his house, but soon afterwards, Chapman had said: 'Mr. and Mrs Ward, allow me to introduce you to my wife, Mrs. Chapman.' He claimed that they had married at a Catholic church in the city. Soon afterwards, they moved to Hastings.

The prosecution next called Detective Sergeant Arthur Neil. He had examined the registers at Somerset House, and found no trace of any marriage between Isabella Spink and, either George Chapman, or Severin Klosowski.

Annie Helsdown had lived with her husband, Frederick, at 10 Hill Street, Hastings. At one stage, Chapman and Isabella had come to lodge at their house and whilst there, he had opened a barber's shop in George Street. By all accounts, the business was a very successful one. It was Chapman who did all the hair-cutting and shaving, but Isabella helped out there. In 1896, however, Isabella fell ill. She had terrible pains in her stomach, and vomited a lot. The vomit always had a greenish tinge.

Martha Doubleday lived in Richmond Street, near Bartholomew Square, and knew the *Prince of Wales* public house there. Chapman had taken the tenancy of the pub in 1897, bringing Isabella Spink with him. Martha and Isabella soon became close friends.

Towards the end of that year, Martha had noticed that Isabella was rather pale and she seemed to lose a lot of weight. Two weeks before Christmas, Chapman approached Martha, and asked her to sit with his wife, as she was very ill in bed. Martha went up to the bedroom to see Isabella, and asked why there was no doctor in attendance. Chapman asked who the nearest doctor was, and one named Rogers was duly sent for.

Over the next few days, Isabella grew steadily worse, despite the ministrations of the doctor. Chapman was most attentive during this time, constantly bringing Isabella brandy but, every time she drank some, Isabella was violently sick immediately afterwards.

As Christmas approached, Isabella's condition grew worse. On one occasion, Martha saw Chapman lean over the bed and say to Isabella: 'Pray God go away from me.' On Christmas Day, Isabella died, but Chapman still opened for business that day.

Jane Mumford had also nursed Isabella in her final illness, taking over from Mrs Doubleday occasionally. She saw

Chapman often administer medicine to his wife, and after each dose she seemed to vomit.

The Dr Rogers referred to by Martha Doubleday and Jane Mumford had, by now, passed away himself but Elizabeth Waymark, a professional nurse, who the doctor sometimes employed, was able to give her testimony. She had been sent, by Dr Rogers, to minister to Isabella in the last two weeks of her life. She too reported that Isabella complained of violent pains in her stomach, and had bouts of sickness which produced green-tinged vomit.

Henry Edward Pierce was an undertaker, and he was called to the Prince of Wales on Christmas Day 1897. The funeral was arranged, and finally took place, on 30 December, at St Patrick's Cemetery, Leytonstone. The coffin had a plate attached to it which read: 'Mary Isabella Chapman, aged 41 years, died December 25th, 1897.' Mr Pierce was present when the coffin was exhumed, in 1902, and was able to identify both the coffin and the body inside, since it was in a remarkably good state of preservation. The fact that antimony is one of the poisons that preserves the flesh, had already been noted by the various doctors involved in the case.

Dr Thomas Stevenson was then recalled. He too had been present at Isabella's exhumation, and later had tested various organs from her body. His opinion was that she had died from antimony poisoning, finding a total of 3.83 grains still in the body. He went on to explain that when a dose of tartar emetic is given, the result is vomiting and much of the poison is then ejected. However, a proportion of the antimony is retained in the body, and repeated doses would cause it to accumulate until the person finally expires.

Finally, the prosecution turned to the death of Elizabeth Taylor. William Taylor told the court that the dead woman had been his sister. He recalled Bessie and Chapman living together as man and wife at the *Prince of Wales*. Later they moved to Bishop's Stortford before returning to London, and taking the lease on the *Monument*.

In December 1900, William heard that his sister was ill. He

went to visit her and found her sick and shrunken, having lost a great deal of weight. Bessie told him that she had terrible stomach pains, and kept being sick. The next he heard of Bessie was when their mother wrote to tell him that she had died. Bessie was buried, on 15 February, in the churchyard in Lymm, Cheshire. William was also present, in 1902, when Bessie's coffin was exhumed and recalled that her body was very well preserved.

The next two witnesses, Elizabeth Anne Painter and Martha Stevens, had both been friends of Bessie, and visited her at the *Monument*. They reported the symptoms that she displayed in the final weeks of her illness; symptoms that corresponded precisely with those displayed by Isabella Spink and Maud Marsh.

Once again, Dr Stevenson had tested organs removed from Bessie Taylor's body. There was antimony present in all the major organs and the various figures gave an estimation that some 29.12 grains of tartar emetic had been administered.

The prosecution case rested. No witnesses were called for the defence, Chapman's counsel choosing to rely instead on the argument that there was no apparent motive for Chapman to have poisoned these three women.

Although evidence had now been given on all three deaths, the jury were only asked to return a verdict in the case of Maud Marsh, the most recent victim. It took them just ten minutes to decide that Chapman was guilty as charged. The death sentence having been given, Chapman had to be supported by two warders before being taken down to the cells.

There was to be no reprieve and, on Tuesday 7 April 1903, George Chapman had to be supported a second time as he stood on the trap in the execution chamber at Wandsworth prison, where he was hanged by William Billington and Henry Pierrepoint.

It was the busiest year of the entire twentieth century for the hangman of Britain, with a total of twenty-seven people, twenty-four men and three women, dying on the gallows.

# Chapter 28

# Albert Bridgeman
## 1905

There were four people lodging on the second floor of the house at 37 Compton Street. In addition to John Ballard and his wife, Catherine, there were also their two daughters, Mary and Elizabeth.

In the early part of 1902, Mary started walking out with a young man named Albert Bridgeman, whose friends called him Alf. The couple fell in love, and were soon engaged to be married. Then, in February, Albert, a soldier, went off to fight in the Boer War. He did not return to England until the end of that same year, and almost immediately, Mary noticed a change in her fiance. Albert had taken to frequenting boxing clubs, a sport Mary did not approve of and, perhaps of more concern, he had taken to drinking rather heavily.

For two more years, Mary tried to maintain the relationship, but it soon became obvious that Albert wasn't going to change. He was no longer the sweet, kind, gentle man, that Mary had first loved. It was for that reason that Mary broke off the engagement, on 27 December 1904. Albert appeared to take it well, though. He remained on good terms with the entire family, and still visited their home from time to time.

One of those visits took place on the evening of Friday 3 March 1905. Albert called at the house, and he and John Ballard sat down together, over a glass of beer. It was a very pleasant night and, in due course, Albert left to return to his own lodgings at 4 Dyott Street, near Shaftesbury Avenue. Soon after this, the Ballard family retired for the night.

At 12.30am on Saturday 4 March, John Ballard was woken by a noise on the landing, outside his bedroom. Thinking they might have burglars, John went to investigate, only to find Albert

Bridgeman, creeping along the hallway. A surprised John said: 'Hello Alf, what are you doing here at this time of night? Your place is at home, not coming here, and frightening me out of my life. You have been drinking. Why don't you go home to your right place?' Albert apologised profusely, and said he would see them tomorrow, actually meaning later that same day. He was then gently escorted from the premises.

At some time between 9.00am and 9.30am that same morning, Saturday 4 March, Albert Bridgeman walked into Walter Sharwood's pawnbroker's establishment, at 183 St John's Street. He was attended to by George Mills, one of the sales assistants, and asked to see a silver chain, that was hanging in the window. Having inspected the item, Albert said he would take it. He then asked to see some silver medals, and purchased two. Next he said he had seen a razor, and wished to look at that too. Another purchase made, Albert then asked Walter if they sold revolvers. Walter replied that the usually did, but they had none in stock at that time. He also mentioned that when any came in, he would need to see Albert's gun licence before he could sell him one. Albert, seemingly happy with his purchases, left the shop.

At 11.30am, Albert was back at 37 Compton Street. The door was opened by Esther Wheeler, who lived on the floor above the Ballards. She explained that all of the Ballards were out. Albert thanked her for her trouble, and walked off down the street.

Where Albert went to next is not known, but by 12.20pm, he had found Catherine Ballard. They were seen drinking together in the *Wheatsheaf* public house, by James Wheeler, Esther's husband.

At 1.00pm Albert and Catherine were seen entering number 37 together. Emily Shadbolt, who lived with Mrs Wheeler on the floor above, saw them go into Catherine's rooms. Minutes later, a bloodcurdling scream rang out. Rushing onto the landing to look over the bannister, Mrs Shadbolt saw Albert leaving the Ballards' rooms. His hands and face were covered in blood, and as he ran down the stairs, he left bloody footprints behind him.

Esther Wheeler had also heard that terrible scream, and as Mrs Shadbolt ran out onto the landing, Esther ran to her front window. She was in time to see Albert leaving the house and she too noticed that his hands were covered in blood. As he left, Albert placed one hand on a gatepost, and a bloody print was left behind. Esther knew that something terrible must have happened downstairs. She pulled on her coat and went to the police station in Hunter Street.

Constable Reuben Roth was on duty at the police station and, having heard Esther Wheeler's story, went with her back to Compton Street. Entering the Ballards' rooms he found Catherine lying on the floor in a bedroom at the back of the house. She was partly beneath the bed, lying face down, and there was a great deal of blood around her body. Constable Roth sent for his inspector, and a doctor.

Dr Thomas Murphy, the Divisional Police Surgeon, arrived at Compton Street at 1.20pm. He confirmed that Catherine Ballard was dead, and then made an initial examination of her body. Dr Murphy noted five deep wounds on Catherine's scalp, all extending down to the bone. These had, almost certainly, been made by a small shovel, found at the scene. This had broken in two. The handle had been thrown onto the bed, and the head lay on the floor, close to Catherine's body. Dr Murphy also noted a large, gaping wound, on the left side of Catherine's throat. This extended down to the spinal column, and had severed all the major veins and arteries.

The search was on for Albert Bridgeman, but he was not seen again until 10.35am on Sunday 5 March. Detective Constable Henry Gallard was in Hunter Street, when he saw Albert walking towards him. Gallard identified himself as a policeman, but, before he could say anything else, Albert replied: 'Yes, I know what it is for. It is for murder. Here is the razor I done [sic] it with.' He then put his hand into his jacket pocket, drew out the still bloodstained razor, and handed it over to Gallard.

Albert appeared at the magistrates' court the following day, Monday 6 March. After he had been remanded he was, once again, placed in the care of Constable Gallard. Albert began to make a statement, and Gallard, quite properly, cautioned him again. Ignoring the caution, Albert said:

The job is done, I know that.

I went to Mrs. Ballard's on Saturday, and intended to make her drunk, and then cut her throat on the bed. I treated her several times, but could not make her drunk, so I took the poker when her back was turned, and was going to strike her, when she looked round and shouted 'Murder!' I then struck her on the head with the poker. She again screamed 'Murder!' but only faintly.

I struck her again, and she fell on the floor. I then took the poker with both hands, and struck her on the head with all the force I could, which was enough to kill a bullock. I then cut her throat and intended to put her under the bed to hide her, wipe the blood up, and wait for her husband. She always is very nice in front of your face, but has being saying a lot about me, and called me a name, which was disgraceful to my mother.

I looked out of the door, and Mrs. Shadbolt looked over the banisters and said, 'Oh, Alf, what have you done? 'I then ran away. Mrs. Shadbolt saved Ballard's life, as I intended to kill him, and then cut my own throat.

Twenty-two-year-old Albert Bridgeman appeared at the Old Bailey on 5 April 1905, to answer a charge of wilful murder. The judge presiding over the case was Mr Justice Jelf. Albert was defended by Mr Cutis Bennett, whilst the case for the Crown was led by Mr Charles Mathews, assisted by Mr Arthur Gill.

John Ballard told the court of his daughter's engagement to Albert, and that the engagement had been broken off by her, at Christmastime the previous year. He also spoke of his encounter with Albert, on the landing outside his bedroom, early on 4 March. He said he knew of no reason why Albert should wish to murder him, or his wife, or any of his family.

Mary Ballard confirmed that she had known Albert for about five years in all, and had ended their engagement, because of his love of pugilism and drink. She was followed to the witness stand by John Ballard's eldest daughter, Alice Elizabeth Cooper, who was married to John and lived at 49 Kenton Street.

Alice had seen Albert a number of times, in the days before he had taken her mother's life. On 28 February, she had seen him between 11.30am and noon, and he was already much the worse for drink. The next day, Wednesday 1 March, she saw him again, and he told her that he had just been to Hounslow, to buy himself out of the Army. That night, Albert had slept at her house. She had a lodger, William Farthing, and he was a close friend of Albert. The two had both come back to Kenton Street very drunk, and Alice had suggested that he stay there that night.

On Friday 3 March, Alice saw Albert for the last time. He was in the public house, across the road from where she lived, and was drinking with William Farthing and her sister, Elizabeth. Once again Albert was much the worse for drink. He seemed to be rambling, and told Alice that he intended to do murder. She advised him to go home to his lodgings, but he went on to say that he intended to murder her mother and father. Unfortunately, Alice thought that this was nothing more than the ramblings of a drunken man.

Elizabeth Ballard agreed with her sister's testimony. She had been in the *Wheatsheaf*, with Albert and William Farthing, on the evening of 3 March. At one stage, Albert went outside to be sick, and she went with him. After he had vomited, Albert said he wanted to buy a revolver and kill her mother, her father, her sister and her. She too thought he was rambling because of the drink.

William Hay was a cab driver, and on 4 March, he had been on a rank in Kenton Street. Albert had approached him, soon after he had killed Catherine, and asked to be taken to the *Mechanic's Larder* pub, on Gray's Inn Road. As they went along Judd Street and Regent Street, Hay looked down into the well of the cab and saw that his fare was hiding on the floor, as if he did not wish to be seen.

On arrival at the *Mechanic's Larder*, Albert invited Hay to join him for a drink, and paid him half a crown for his fare, much more than was actually owed. Seeing that he had a most generous customer, Hay agreed to the drink and they each had a Scotch. Hay testified that he saw no signs of blood, anywhere on Albert's person.

Martha Palmer was Albert's landlady in Dyott Street. She testified that he had lived at her address for two years. She had last seen him at around 7.00am on 4 March, when he came home in a most excited mood. He could not sit, or stand still, but paced around the room. He asked for a cup of tea, but would not wait whilst the kettle boiled. Finally, he asked her to make him some toast, but only ate one corner of it.

Perhaps the most damaging evidence came from Inspector Walter Dew, the man who would catch Crippen in five years time. On 4 March, he had gone to Albert's lodgings and searched them. He found, amongst other things, a small cash box. In that box there were two letters, both written by the prisoner.

In the first of those letters, Albert had written:

Carefully read this. I hereby leave £5 to Mrs. Palmer, the rest of my property to my dear mother. Determined to swing. My watch and chain, to William Farthing, my pal. My medal to Mrs. Palmer, if I succeed in murdering Mrs. Ballard. God bless those who have done good to me.

The second letter read:

I have been utterly deceived, by those who I have tried to do good to, as sure as God is my judge. Utter strangers have told me all about this wicked bitch. When the time comes for God to call me away I am prepared to die. 4th of March, 1905, A. Bridgman.

Albert's defence was a combination of drink and insanity. He claimed, first of all, that he had drunk so much, that he could remember nothing of what he had done. Allied to this was the fact that whilst he had been in South Africa, in 1902, a large, heavy piece of iron had fallen onto his head in one of the blockhouses. Ever since then he had suffered from terrible headaches, and blackouts. None of this, however, impressed the jury who took just a few minutes to deliberate before returning their guilty verdict.

Sentenced to death, Albert Bridgeman was hanged at Pentonville on Wednesday 26 April 1905, by John Billington and Henry Pierrepoint.

# Chapter 29

# Charles Henry Rogers and Jessie Elizabeth Lucas

# 1907

ohn Smith was a bully. For four years he had lived with Jessie Lucas, at 41 Northdown Street, and for the last three of those years, he had beaten her on a regular basis. About the only person Jessie had to turn to, was her brother, Charles Rogers.

Some time in late May 1907, Charles paid a visit to Jessie's home, and spoke to her landlady, Amelia Barber. Charles asked: 'How does that man treat my sister?' Amelia, who had never actually witnessed any of the beatings, and didn't really wish to get involved, replied: 'Very well, as far as I know.' Charles was not to be mollified and continued: 'He has been knocking her about, and a fortnight ago she came to me with a black eye that he had given her. I have cautioned him, that if he ever raises his hand to my sister again, he is a dead man. I will kill him and leave him stone dead.' Jessie Lucas, who was present during this conversation, then put her arms around her brother's neck and remarked: 'He deserves it, Charlie.'

The warning Charles Rogers had given to John Smith, was not heeded. Smith continued to beat his common-law wife, and she continued to sport bruises and marks upon her face and body. Things finally came to a head on Sunday 16 June 1907.

At 1.35pm on that date, John Smith was drinking with some friends, in the *Albion* public house, at 33 Caledonian Road, Islington. What precisely took place that afternoon, would depend on which particular witnesses were believed. What is undoubtedly true is that, at around 2.40pm, Charles Rogers and his sister walked into the bar and, after a few words had been exchanged, Charles struck Smith on the point of his jaw. As Smith fell backwards, onto the shoulder of the gentleman sitting next to him, Charles struck him for a second time. Then, as Smith lay on the floor, apparently unconscious, a satisfied Smith walked out of the *Albion*, taking his long-suffering sister with him.

Unfortunately, John Smith was not merely unconscious. When his friends failed to wake him, the doctor was called and he pronounced life to be extinct. Both Charles and Jessie were arrested, and charged with manslaughter.

The two defendants appeared at the Old Bailey on 22 July 1907, before Mr Justice Darling. Asked how they wished to plead, Charles replied that he was guilty as charged. Jessie entered a plea of not guilty, meaning that the evidence would have to be heard. The case for the Crown was then led by Mr Arthur Gill, who was assisted by Mr Graham-Campbell. Jessie was defended by Mr Arnold Ward.

Amelia Barber, in addition to detailing the conversation she had had with Charles, when he had threatened John Smith's life, also referred to a conversation she had overheard, at least in part, at 6.40am on 16 June, the day Smith had been killed. There was some sort of argument, during which Smith insisted that Jessie should go back upstairs to their rooms. Jessie had refused and Smith had made some remark about her face, which Amelia did not catch. She did, however, hear Jessie's reply quite clearly. She had said: 'I am not ashamed of my face. I am going to follow you, and the first copper I meet, I will have you charged.' They both then left the house.

Something of the behaviour of John Smith was detailed by the next witness. George Shears also lived at 41 Northdown Street, and at around 10.00pm on Saturday 15 June, he had been talking to Jessie, when John Smith came up behind her. Without saying a word, Smith struck Jessie, with his clenched fist, in her mouth and on her cheek. George saw no other reason for this, apart from the fact that he was talking to her. and Smith didn't like it.

The time came for witnesses from the Albion to be heard. The first of these was Arthur Williams, a friend of Smith's, who had been drinking with him, in the pub, from 1.35pm on June 16th.

At 2.00pm, Charles and Jessie had walked in, and strode up to where Smith was sitting. Jessie had said that she had brought her brother to give him a good hiding, and Arthur noticed that her face and lip were badly discoloured. Charles immediately shouted: 'What did you come to my house for last night, you fucking bastard? I have a good mind to put your lights out.' To this, Smith had apparently simply replied: 'I wish for no trouble.' He then stood, walked to the end of the bar, purchased a packet of cigarettes and lit one.

Charles marched over to where Smith now stood, and threatened him again. Jessie had also gone forward and she commented: 'When we return you may have your jaw broken and a few ribs broken, and then you can go to the hospital and rot you old bastard.' With that, Charles and Jessie left the bar.

At 2.40pm, they were back. Charles again marched up to where Smith was sitting and said: 'You are still here Mr fucking Smith, I have a good mind to out you.' Charles then raised his right hand and struck Smith on the point of his jaw. This was followed, as Smith fell backwards, with a left-handed punch to the side of the head. As Smith fell to the floor, Charles strode towards the main door and said: 'You have got it you old bleeder.' He and Jessie then left together. Minutes later, Arthur was running off to fetch the doctor.

The testimony given by Arthur Williams did not agree with that of other witnesses to the events of that afternoon. Edward Litton was also in the bar. He did not hear Jessie Lucas say anything at all.

Arthur Bell was another customer, and he agreed that Charles had said something about Smith going to see his landlady, Mrs Leonard, but no threats were made, no foul language was used, and Jessie did not speak at all.

Medical evidence was given by Dr Richard Lawrence Caunter. He had been called out to the *Albion*, by Arthur Williams, and arrived there at about 3.00pm. By this time, John Smith had been laid out along a bench. Dr Caunter examined him, and confirmed that he was dead. There were some small marks on his lip and on the angle of his jaw, on the left-hand side. Dr Caunter believed that the blows Smith had received, were the direct cause of death.

Inspector Andrew King, along with Sergeant Selby, had gone to Jessie's lodgings at 41 Northdown Street, to arrest her, at 7.30pm. Told that she was being taken in for questioning, Jessie made a dash to pick up a cut-throat razor, saying that she wished to end it all now. She was restrained by the inspector, and taken to King's Cross police station. Told that she would be arrested for causing the death of John Smith an incredulous Jessie cried: 'You do not mean to say he is dead? He had been knocking me about all night, and I went with my brother to fight him. He only got one blow. He cannot be dead.'

The final person into the witness box was Jessie Lucas herself. She told the court that she had one child, a dear son, but should have had two more. She had been pregnant on two other occasions, but had lost both babies due to Smith's brutal treatment of her.

Jessie told the court of the blows she had received on 15 June, when she was talking to George Shears. She then went on to say what had happened earlier in the day of 16 June.

She and Smith had gone out for a drink together, and on the way home, as they passed the butcher who Jessie dealt with each week, she gave him a polite hello. Smith immediately gave her two more blows. She had run off to tell two policemen, who happened to be in the vicinity, but they simply told her to go home, and report him at the station if he hit her again.

At around noon that same day, she had decided to go out, and get herself a glass of beer. On the way, she met her brother, quite by accident and, seeing the marks and bruises on her face, he had asked if Smith had been beating her again. Anxious to avoid trouble, she had lied and said that she had a bad toothache. Charles didn't believe her, and advised her to have Smith arrested and charged. He then invited Jessie to go for a drink with him.

As they enjoyed a glass of ale in a local public house, Smith looked in at the window. Believing that Jessie was with another man, he stormed in, at which point Charles turned and said: 'You have caught her with the wrong one. You know me.' Smith had then called Jessie a foul name, and walked out of the pub.

After finishing their drinks, Charles and Jessie had walked off together until, by chance, they found themselves close to the *Albion* and decided to have another glass. Smith was already in there. She had said nothing to him. She had certainly not said that she had brought her brother to give him a good hiding.

The jury deliberated for a short time before returning with their verdict. They had come to believe that John Smith was indeed a man who beat his wife regularly, and that she had suffered at his hands for years. They therefore returned a guilty verdict, but added that they believed she had acted under the greatest provocation, and that they wished to give the strongest possible recommendation to mercy.

Mr Justice Darling, it seemed, agreed completely with that verdict. Taking into account Charles guilty plea, Jessie's suffering, and the jury's recommendation, he sentenced both of the prisoners to a token three days in prison. As they had both already served more than that time in custody, this meant that they could be released immediately.

# Chapter 30

# Walter Edward Fensham
# 1908

ames Christy Fensham had been married twice. His first marriage had taken place in 1862 and his wife had borne him no fewer than twelve children and, by all accounts, had been a most placid and kind woman. The same, however, could not be said for his second wife, Harriett Mary Clarke, who he married in the last quarter of 1903. The new Mrs Clarke had something of a temper, and often misused her husband, usually by showing him no respect, drinking rather heavily, and even physically attacking him. This did not please James's children, especially one of his sons, Walter Edward.

In 1903, at the time of his father's new marriage, Walter lived with the newlyweds at their lodgings, at 15 St James Road. Very soon afterwards, though, after seeing how his father was being treated, Walter moved to fresh lodgings at Rowton House in King's Cross Road, but often visited the family home. One such visit was made on Saturday 28 December 1907.

It was 8.00pm when Walter reached St James Road. At the time, Harriett was in the kitchen and, seeing her guest arrive, offered to cook him a pork chop, which she then proceeded to do. James was also in the kitchen, and chatted to his son, whilst the meal was being prepared. Once the chop was served, though, James left the room to do some shopping. It was then some time between 8.15pm and 8.30pm.

After finishing his shopping, James returned to the house and went into the front parlour to talk to his landlord, the gentleman who actually owned the house and also lived there. James was thinking of relocating and the two men discussed the forthcoming move. During that conversation, James heard his son shout, from the kitchen; Good night father. James went out into the hallway to see Walter out and then, once Walter had walked out into the cold night air, James went back into the kitchen, in answer to a call from his daughter, Florence Louise, who also lodged at the house.

Though he had heard no shouting, no struggle and no noise of any kind, it was clear that something terrible had happened in that kitchen. Harriett Mary Fensham lay on the floor, a knife embedded in her throat. Florence managed to say that Walter had done it, before she dashed from the room to get help. James crouched down and cradled his wife in his arms. He then removed the knife, and threw it down onto a nearby table top.

Florence had run to yet another lodger at the house, Gertrude Sutherland. She went down to the kitchen, with Florrie, and saw the terrible scene for herself. James was still cradling his wife in his arms, and trying to revive her. It was Gertrude who had the presence of mind to call for the police and a doctor.

It was around 9.15pm, when Dr Robert James Harbinson arrived at 15 St James Road. Harriett was still alive. She was unconscious, and her pulse was very weak indeed. Dr Harbinson managed to stitch the gaping wound in her throat before sending Harriett to hospital.

It was Dr Rubens Wade, who attended to Harriett at the Great Northern Hospital. By the time she was admitted it was close to 10.15pm. Dr Wade noted that the wound, on the left side of the neck, had started to bleed again so removed the stitches Dr Harbinson had made and attended to an injury to the jugular vein. Harriett did not recover consciousness, though, and at 6.15am on 29 December, she died.

Meanwhile, on the night of the attack, the police were busy looking for Walter Edward Fensham. They began by visiting his lodgings, but he had not returned there after leaving his father's house. In fact, Walter had gone to 3 Granville Place, the residence of one of his brothers, William Joseph Fensham.

When Walter arrived at his brother's house, he was very excitable, and William noticed that there was blood on one of his hands. 'What have you done?' enquired William. Walter replied: 'I must have struck her with my knife. I have done it. I have done

the old woman in. Let's come upstairs and have a bit of supper.'
William, seeing the state that Walter was in, refused to let him
into the house. At this, Walter suggested: 'Well, if I cannot come
upstairs and have some supper, will you come out and have a
drink?' William then went out with Walter but, on the corner of
the street, said that he believed that Walter had already had too
much to drink, and was too excitable for more.

Walter then said he was going to go to the police and give
himself up, but William noticed that he was walking instead
towards his lodgings at Rowton House. Walter suggested he
should go to bed, and they would talk again in the morning,
when he was feeling better. From there, William immediately
went to his father's house to check out the truth of what Walter
had said. Finding that Harriett had indeed been attacked, and
was now fighting for her life, William then went to the police
himself and told them that Walter had now returned to his
lodgings. He was arrested there, in the early hours of the
morning.

Walter Fensham's trial for murder opened on 4 February
1908 and was to last until 6 February. During the three days of
the proceedings, Walter was defended by Mr Danford Thomas.
The case for the prosecution was led by Sir Charles Mathews,
who was assisted by Mr RF Graham-Campbell.

James Christy Fensham told the court what had happened on
Saturday 28 December, but he also confirmed that his son had
some rather bad health problems. Walter had been receiving
treatment for some time, and had been in a number of hospitals.

Florence Fensham said that she had left Walter and Harriett
alone in the kitchen, at around 6.00pm, and had gone upstairs
to see Mrs Sutherland. When she came downstairs again she saw
that Harriett and Walter were enjoying a glass of beer together.
They were still in the kitchen and no sooner had Florence
arrived in the room than her brother said 'Will you go upstairs
Florrie?' Florence thought this was some kind of joke and said:
'Give me a chance, I have only just come down.'

At this point, Harriett said: 'Will you go home Wally?' Walter
was silent for a few moments and then replied: 'Well, if you

don't want me, I will go home and then stood to leave. Walter did not leave, though, he walked over to where Florence stood and whispered to her: 'I don't care if I do get hung for poor father.' Then, as if to emphasise that he was being serious, he showed Florence a knife he had in his pocket.

Florence still wasn't sure if Walter was joking, and told him not to be so foolish. She did not go back upstairs, but watched as Walter sat down next to his step-mother, seized her by the throat and then plunged the knife into her. He then stood, walked calmly to the door, and shouted good night to his father. Florence was shocked into silence for a minute of so but then the horror of what she had just witnessed gave her back her voice and she screamed out for help.

After Gertrude Sutherland and William Fensham had given their evidence, the prosecution called the medical witnesses. Dr Harbinson spoke of his visit to St James Road, and of seeing a wound some four inches long and an inch and a half wide. Although he ordered that Harriett be taken to the hospital, Dr Harbinson had been convinced at the time that she would not recover from such a wound.

Dr Wade told of his treating the injured woman, on her arrival at the hospital, and of her death the following morning. He had since examined the knife, which had been found half-open on the kitchen table. It was an old knife, and quite difficult to open out. The blade was very blunt, so it would have required a great deal of force to inflict the wound which Harriett had suffered.

Details of Walter's arrest were then given. Sergeant George Osborn had gone to Rowton House with the prisoner's brother, William. There he found Walter asleep in bed, and having roused him heard Walter say: 'Is she dead?' At that time, Harriett was still alive, so Osborn informed Walter that he was wanted on a charge of attempted murder. On the way to the police station Walter observed: 'I will hang for her; she has ruined my father.'

Taken to the Caledonian Road police station, Walter was interviewed and charged by Inspector Arthur Neil. In reply to the charge of attempted murder, Walter replied: 'I was there. I do not know what I did. I will say nothing.' Later, when the charge was amended to one of murder, Walter said: ' I did not intend to do it. Do you think I shall get hung for it? I went there last night. She called me a bastard, and said I only came there to get what I could out of the old man. I lost my temper.'

Walter Fensham stepped into the witness box to give his own version of events.

He began by saying that he had lived with his father until his remarriage. He went on to say that at the age of twenty-three, he had started working for the London Omnibus Carriage Company, and while with them, he had fallen off a horse. He had injured himself badly, and still had a large lump on the back of his head. Since then he had been in St Bartholomew's Hospital two or three times, and had been operated on twice. He had also been in Holborn Infirmary at various times from 1903 to 1907, and in the Royal Free Hospital. Walter went on to say that he still had terrible pains in his head, and to relive that pain, had taken laudanum every day.

Continuing his evidence, Walter said that he had been drinking heavily on the day before he had attacked Harriett. As a result, he felt very bad on the morning of Saturday 28 December. That afternoon, he had enjoyed a single drink with his father, in the *Montrose* public house and after separating from him, went on to the *Pocock Arms*, where he had quite a few drinks, before returning to the *Montrose*. It was from there that he walked to his father's house.

Turning to the actual attack, Walter said that he vaguely remembered having something to eat. He remembered his sister, Florence, being in the kitchen with him and Harriett, and might have suggested that she go upstairs to fetch Mrs Sutherland down so that she could join them in a drink. When Florence had left the room, Harriett had jumped up and said something like: 'You are only a bastard and come here to get what you can out of your father.' After that, all he could remember was seizing her. He had no recollection of using a knife on her.

Other witnesses were called to prove some of what Walter had said. Charles Crew had seen him drinking in the *Montrose* on 28 December, and thought him much the worse for drink.

James Smith, a chemist, of Gray's Inn Road, confirmed that Walter had been visiting his shop for some weeks, to purchase laudanum. Finally, Dr William John Guiseppi, a surgeon at the Royal Free Hospital, confirmed the various operations and treatments Walter had received. He had been suffering from tuberculous glands in his neck. These would have caused him a lot of pain, and the effect of the laudanum he was taking to relieve that pain, could well make him less responsible for his actions, especially when he was excited.

Having heard all the testimony, the jury returned the verdict that Walter was guilty of murder but added a recommendation to mercy on account of his health problems and the stress of his father's ill-treatment at the hands of Harriett. There could, however, only be one sentence and Walter was sentenced to death.

Walter Fensham did not hang. The recommendation of the jury was heeded and, in due course, his sentence was commuted to one of life imprisonment.

# Chapter 31

# Arthur Robert Canham
## 1924

There were problems at 22 Mitford Road, and most of them seemed to be due to the efforts, or rather the lack of effort, of the titular head of the household, Arthur Robert Canham.

Over the last five years, Canham had only worked for some twenty-six weeks in total. He managed to scrape by on a small pension of £8 every couple of months, the household income being supplemented by the wages his wife, Selina, earned as a cleaner to a private house, and what his sixteen-year-old son, also named Arthur, managed to earn. Canham made up any other shortfall by selling articles which belonged to his wife, and this led to numerous arguments between them. So tense had the atmosphere become inside number 22, that Canham slept in one bedroom at the back, whilst his wife and four children shared the other bedroom, at the front of the house.

On Thursday 6 November 1924, Arthur James Charles Canham, the sixteen year old who was the eldest child, rose around 7.00am and readied himself for work. Selina made Arthur his breakfast, and whilst he was eating it, his father came into the kitchen. For once, there were no cross words between them and, when Arthur left for work at 7.25am, all was well in the house.

The second child was eleven-year-old Winifred Maud Canham. She got out of bed soon after her brother had left for work, and helped her mother get the two youngest children ready for school. All three children had their breakfast and, by the time they left for school together, at 8.45am, Selina was in the kitchen, tidying the breakfast things away whilst their father, Arthur, was in the front room reading a newspaper.

At 12.20pm, Winifred and the two youngest children arrived home for lunch. At first, there seemed to be no-one else in the house. Winifred assumed that her mother had gone to her cleaning job, and that her father was out somewhere or other, so she got lunch for herself and the other two children. When the meal was almost ready, Winifred went upstairs to fetch a tablecloth.

It seemed that Arthur Canham was home after all. His bedroom door was closed, but Winifred could hear him moving about inside and heard him say: 'Wake up! Wake up! Get to work.' She then noticed that something seemed to have been placed against the bottom of the bedroom door, blocking off any light coming from within. Her curiosity aroused, Winifred then returned to the kitchen and noticed, for the first time, that the floor had recently been washed, but there were still smears of what looked like blood, close to the kitchen sink.

By now, Winifred was certain that something bad had happened in the house. An intelligent girl, she did not wish to alarm the younger children so escorted them back to school, once they had finished eating. Winifred, though, did not go to school. She went to the house where her mother cleaned, confirmed that she had not arrived that day, told the lady of the house what she had seen and heard back at Mitford Road, and asked her to go to the police station with her.

Winifred went to the Hornsey Road police station, and told her story to the officer on duty. She then handed over her front door key, and waited at the station, whilst officers were sent to investigate.

It was Constable Frank Parker and Constable Ivey, who were sent to 22 Mitford Road. They arrived at 2.30pm, to find the house securely locked. That was no problem, however, as Winifred had provided the key. The two officers entered the house and began by searching the rooms downstairs.

There was no sign of either Arthur Canham or Selina, his wife, but the officers did note the apparent smears of blood on parts of the kitchen floor. They then began to look upstairs.

It was Parker who first heard the low groaning from the back bedroom. The door was locked but Parker kicked it open. Once inside, he and Ivey found Canham lying on his bed. He had attached a rubber tube to the gas tap in the room and placed the other end inside his mouth. The room smelled strongly of gas and it was clear that Canham was trying to kill himself. Constable Ivey opened the bedroom window to let the gas out and some fresh air in, whilst Parker tore the tube from Canham's mouth, before contacting the police station for reinforcements, and the local doctor.

Whilst waiting for the doctor to arrive, Constable Parker began a quick search of the bedroom. He noticed that in one corner of the room, there was a cupboard, and its door was bulging open. There seemed to be something blocking it from the inside. Taking a closer look, Parker saw what looked like a human knee. Removing some items of clothing, very carefully, Parker found Selina Canham. She was lying on her back, with her knees tucked up and her head leaning forward. There was a good deal of blood about her head and upper body.

Dr Fraser was the first medical practitioner on the scene. He confirmed that Selina was dead, and noted a number of circular wounds upon the top of her head. In due course, the Divisional Police Surgeon, Dr Sidney John Rowntree arrived. By this time, Arthur Canham had largely recovered from the gas inhalation, but he still seemed to be rather disorientated at the site of so many police and medical men in his bedroom.

Taken to the police station for questioning, Canham admitted that he had killed his wife. He claimed that they had argued after he had complained that she had not made him any breakfast. He had then found two hammers and, taking the smaller one, had struck her on the head a number of times. Rather callously, at one stage he remarked; I only used a small hammer. It was lying on top of the dresser.

Canham appeared at the Old Bailey on 15 December 1924, before Mr Justice Shearman. The case for the prosecution was detailed by Mr Travers Humphreys whilst Canham was defended by Mr Fox-Davies.

Annie Sarah Truscott lived at 14 Cornwallis Road, also in

Islington, and she was the dead woman's sister. She confirmed that Selina had often complained to her that her husband did not provide enough to maintain the children, but had never complained of violence from her husband.

Sixteen-year-old Arthur Canham told a different story, though. He had seen many arguments between his mother and father and some of these had come to blows. On 30 October, for example, he had seen his father grab his mother by the throat and try to strangle her. This was because she had objected, after discovering that he had just sold her phonograph. It was with much difficulty that Selina managed to struggle free.

Further medical evidence was given by Dr Rowntree, who had performed the post-mortem on 9 November. He found five wounds on the top of Selina's head, all of which had penetrated down to the bone. There was a linear fracture at the base of the skull, and this was the direct cause of death.

Perhaps the most telling evidence was the statement Canham had made at the police station. In this he admitted to striking Selina on the head, whilst she was in the kitchen. He was surprised that there was only a little blood and he washed this up with a cloth before going upstairs and finding the rubber tube he intended to use to take his own life. Going back downstairs he collected Selina's body, stuffed it into the cupboard and covered her over with some clothes. He then partly undressed before lying down on his bed, switching on the gas and placing the rubber tube into his mouth. The next things he knew, someone was shaking him awake and the room was full of strange people, some of them in police uniforms.

After a short deliberation, the jury announced that they had found Canham guilty of murder, and he was sentenced to death. An appeal was heard on 12 January 1925, but the judges ruled that there was nothing in it and the death sentence was confirmed.

However, before the execution could be carried out, the Home Office announced that they had decided to commute Canham's sentence to one of life imprisonment.

# Chapter 32

# James Lucas
## 1929

ohn Francis Warden was a bricklayer and, in October 1929, was working as part of a gang on a premises in Islington. On 12 October, the gang finished work at noon and John, along with one of his fellow workmen, Francis Edward Marden, decided to go for a few drinks.

Their first port of call was a public house in Amwell Street, where both men had just one pint. From there they walked to a second pub, on the corner of Penton Street, then on to a third establishment in White Lion Street, where they finally finished drinking at around 2.50pm. It was now time to return home, and the two friends started walking towards Godson Street, where Warden lived at number 2.

It was in Godson Street, close to Warden's home, where the two men met up with James Lucas, a man who they both knew, though just as an acquaintance. Someone suggested that the three men should play coin tossing for money. The game was duly started, and did not end until around 4.30pm, by which time Lucas had lost almost all of his money.

A very saddened Lucas announced that he had lost £2 5s and, since Marden seemed to have taken most of this, Lucas suggested that he should, at the very least, buy him a drink now. Marden refused, and then he and Warden started walking towards Chapel Street. At this stage, neither man noticed that Lucas was following them.

A few feet further on, Lucas announced his presence, by asking Marden for a penny, so that he could pay his fare home. This time Marden agreed and he and Warden then watched, as Lucas walked away from them. The two work colleagues then stood on the street, conversing for a few more minutes.

At one stage, Warden thought he heard a noise and looked away from his friend. Then, as he had his face turned away from Marden, Warden heard a shuffling noise. He turned back towards Marden and saw, to his horror, that blood was now spurting from his throat. Lucas was behind Marden and walked calmly off as Marden fell to the ground.

John Warden panicked at the sight of all that blood and ran home to 2 Godson Street to tell his mother what had happened. Warden immediately dashed outside, saw for herself what had happened, and then called for her son to bring out a towel. Once John had done this, she tried her best to staunch the bleeding, and stayed with the injured man, until the police and a doctor were in attendance.

Constable Harry Edward Merritt was on duty at the corner of White Conduit Street and Chapel Street, when he heard about the attack in Godson Street. He arrived there at around 4.50pm, and then rang for an ambulance from a nearby call box. Once the ambulance arrived, Merritt went in it, with the injured man, to the Royal Free Hospital.

Dr Margery Edna Roberts was the doctor on duty in the casualty department of the hospital but by the time Marden arrived there, he was already dead. Dr Roberts noted a deep cut on the right side of Marden's neck. She also noted that the right carotid artery and the jugular vein were both cut through.

James Lucas had not got very far. He had merely gone to his brother-in-law's house, at 15 Church Lane, and it was there that he was arrested by the police, at 6.30pm that same evening. He was escorted to King's Cross Road police station, where he was formally charged with murder. In reply to the charge he said: 'I remember nothing.'

The trial of James Lucas took place on 12 November 1929, before Mr Justice Talbot. The prosecution vase was outlined by Mr H D Roome, assisted by Mr G B McClure. Lucas was defended by Mr H Fearnley-Whittingstall.

John Henry Lane was Lucas's brother-in-law, and it was to his house that Lucas had run after the attack. He was rather breathless when he arrived, and seemed to be very excited. He would only say that he had been in some trouble in Chapel

Street, adding that there had been a bit of a tiff. He had been there for about forty-five minutes when the police arrived to take him into custody.

Lane went on to say, however, that Lucas appeared to have some rather severe mental health problems. He had been receiving treatment for epilepsy at St Bartholomew's Hospital for the past six months. He suffered badly from fits, and on many occasions, whilst he had been involved in a conversation, his eyes would suddenly glaze over and he would end up collapsing onto the floor. When he woke up, he would have no recollection of anything that had happened before the attack.

Henry Marden was the next person who stepped into the witness box, but only to give basic details about his son. He explained that Francis had been twenty-seven years old when he died. It had been Henry who made the formal identification at the mortuary.

After John Francis Warden had told his story about the coin gambling, and Lucas's later attack upon Marden, Constable Merritt took the stand. After telling the court of the abortive trip to the hospital with the stricken man, Merritt explained that he had later searched the dead man's pockets. He had found three £1 notes, two ten shilling notes, eight shillings in silver and seven pence in bronze. Much of that money, it was later shown, had belonged to the prisoner at the bar.

Detective Sergeant Peter Beveridge had been the officer who went to 15 Church Lane, to arrest Lucas. On the way to the police station, Lucas seemed to show little understanding of why he had been placed under arrest and at one stage said: 'I know nothing.'

At the police station, Lucas was seen by Detective Inspector John Coles. At 9.20pm, he charged the prisoner with murder, to which Lucas replied: 'I don't remember nothing [sic].' When he was searched, only one halfpenny was found on Lucas. There was no knife or razor and, indeed, none had been found since. Although he had been questioned about it, Lucas could not remember what he had done with the weapon. Finally, Inspector Coles was able to confirm that on the day after his arrest, 13

October, Lucas had suffered a severe fit in the cells, and had to receive urgent medical treatment.

Details were given of Lucas's past life. He had been in the Army, and although he had received a good discharge, he had never seemed to be the same since. He worked for the London Midland and Scottish Railway, at St Pancras and, originally, was given the job of driving carts around the platform. After a number of minor accidents, during which he blanked out and received minor injuries, he was given lighter duties.

There could be no doubt that James Lucas had taken the life of Francis Edward Marden, but it was equally clear that he had some severe health problems, and often had no idea what he had done, especially in times of excitement or stress. It was this which caused the jury to return the verdict that Lucas was guilty of murder, but had been insane at the time he committed the crime.

Spared the death penalty, Lucas was then sentenced to be detained until His Majesty's pleasure be known.

# Chapter 33

# Frederick Williams
# 1931

Although they lived just around the corner from each other, there was bad blood between forty-nine-year-old Frederick Williams and his cousin. Frederick lived at 27 Church Lane, Islington, whilst his cousin, Amelia Gazzard, lived at 6 Rothery Street, and was involved with a man named Edward Ackland, who was known in the district as Ted Burns. Ackland had something of a reputation for violence, and was certainly a figure that anyone would readily recognise, for he only had one eye.

On Friday 31 July 1931, Amelia Gazzard had an argument with Frederick's wife. It was all over nothing, but it didn't help the already strained relationship between the two families. Things were not helped when, at 11.00pm that same night, Amelia saw Frederick outside his house, and called him some rather rude names. Frederick retaliated by punching his cousin in the face.

At some time early the next morning, Saturday 1 August, Edward Ackland, who lodged at 26 Langton Road, called on Amelia and heard the story of her altercation with Williams. Not one to let this matter lie, Edward marched Amelia around to Williams house to find him, once again, at his front door. Once again harsh words were exchanged, and the argument ended with Ackland saying that he would do for Williams that very night.

Frederick Williams spent most of that day in town, but at 10.00pm he was, yet again, standing at his front door, when Ackland returned. This time there was no conversation. Ackland simply lashed out, throwing punches and kicks at Williams, who retaliated. There was a brief fight, during which both men ended up rolling on the ground until, finally, Ackland pulled himself to his feet and walked off towards Amelia's house.

What happened next would vary depending on which story people believed. The upshot was that Williams followed Ackland, and that the fight continued at the end of the street. It ended when Williams pulled out a razor and pulled it across the back of Ackland's neck. What is certain is that Williams must have known that he had hurt Ackland quite badly, because he did not return home immediately. Instead he walked to Islington Green, where he jumped onto a tramcar and went to Holborn. There he had a drink in the *Bull* public house before returning to Church Lane. There Williams discovered that Ackland had been rushed to hospital and the police had called at his home, wishing to speak to him.

Believing that he would be facing no more than a charge of assault, Williams then walked to Islington police station, where he identified himself to Sergeant Alfred Willis. Williams did not try to hide the fact that he had cut Ackland, saying: 'He came at me first. I did not cut him with a razor. It must have been done with the bottle he had, when we had a fight. He struck at me with a bottle and I hit him.'

Unfortunately for Williams, Ackland did not respond to medical treatment. Taken to the hospital, he was seen by Dr Lois Munro at 11.00pm on the night of 1 August. She stitched the deep wound on the back of his neck, during which time she found and removed a small piece of steel, such as that which might have come from an open razor. Ackland remained conscious for about two hours, then slipped into a coma. He was given a blood transfusion but died at 2.40am on 2 August. Williams, still in his police cell, was roused soon afterwards, and told that he was now facing a charge of murder.

Frederick Williams' trial took place on 9 September 1931. The prosecution case was detailed by Mr Eustace Fulton, who was assisted by Mr Gerald Dodson. Williams was defended by Mr Martin O'Connor.

One of the early witnesses was George Robert Gazzard, Amelia's fifteen-year-old son. He said that he had seen Ted

Burns, the name by which he knew the dead man, go towards his mother's house. He was followed by the prisoner, and the two men started to fight in the street. One of the men was carrying either a glass or a bottle and this fell during the struggle and smashed on the pavement.

At this point, Williams left the scene, but returned just a few minutes later. George warned Ackland of his approach and, once again, the two men met in the middle of the road. A second fight began and then George saw a flash of light on a blade of some sort. Ackland then staggered backwards, bleeding badly from a wound on the back of his neck. George immediately ran off to find a police officer.

Constable Charles Bailey was, in fact, further up the street at the time that the fight erupted for the second time. He saw one of the two men collapse to the ground and ran to see what assistance he could give. He found Ackland lying on the ground. in a pool of blood, and arranged for an ambulance to take him to the Royal Free Hospital.

Dr Bernard Henry Spilsbury had performed the post-mortem on Ackland, on 3 August. He reported a deep wound across the back of Ackland's neck and a second, superficial wound, on his right arm. The wound on the neck began behind the right ear, extended all the way around the back, and ended on Ackland's left cheek. It was almost down to the spinal column at the deepest part. Death had been caused by the amount of blood lost.

Rebecca Ackland was the dead man's wife. She lived at 51 Trego Road, Hackney Wick and stated that she and Ackland were separated. They had not lived together for twelve years. Rebecca might well have greatly improved Williams' chances of escaping the noose, when she told the court that her husband had been a very violent man and had started many fights with other men.

A statement Williams had made, when charged with murder was then read out in court. In that he claimed again that the fight had all been down to Ackland, and denied that he had used a razor on the man. He ended his statement with the words: 'I had no intention of killing Ted. I had never had a row with him before. That is all I have to say.'

The jury had a number of points to ponder. The medical evidence of Dr Munro showed that some kind of metallic blade had been used to inflict the wound on Ackland. Tests had shown that the smashed bottle, found at the scene, bore no traces of blood and also that the individual pieces were not sharp enough to cause such a wound. Against that, they had to balance the fact that whilst Williams had taken Ackland's life, the latter had, almost certainly, started the fight. It was, perhaps, those points that led them to return the verdict that William was not guilty of murder, but was guilty of manslaughter.

For Frederick Williams, that verdict meant that a term of imprisonment replaced the hangman's noose.

# Chapter 34

# Frederick George Murphy
## 1937

Wednesday 12 May 1937, was a day of celebration throughout the United Kingdom, for it was Coronation Day for King George VI and his wife, Queen Mary. The entire nation enjoyed a public holiday. Many businesses, especially in London, were closed on that day, and the next, and only due to re-open on Friday 14 May.

Stanley Herbert Wilton, was a salesman for a furniture company, based at 22 Islington Green and, early on the Friday morning, he received a visitor, Ethel May Marshall, who handed him a note. The note read, in part:

> Dear Stan,
> Don't get frighten [sic] there is a dead woman in number 22 and you can believe me, Stan. It [sic] nothing to do with me, but you know what the police will say.

The note ended with:

> Stan you can believe me. I don't know anything about how this woman got in the cellar of number 22.

Stanley hadn't been down in the shop cellar since 5 May, and, thinking that the note was a joke in very poor taste indeed, went to check for himself. There, in the cellar, hidden behind a trunk, was the body of a woman. Stanley immediately called in the police. Fortunately for the investigation, Stanley Wilton was able to tell the police exactly who had written the note. He knew that Ethel Marshall was the girlfriend of fifty-three-year-old Frederick George Murphy, a man employed by the company as an odd-job man.

Dr Sydney Boyd Faulkner arrived at the shop at 11.30am, and

made his initial examination of the body. He estimated that she had been dead for at least twenty-four hours, possibly longer, and noticed that there was a bruise, beneath the point of the woman's chin, another on her neck, and that the left side of her face was swollen. Though it looked as though she might have been struck, the cause of death appeared to be strangulation, though that would need to be confirmed at the post-mortem. That post-mortem was duly carried out by Sir Bernard Spilsbury, who confirmed that death had been due to strangulation. The cricoid and hyoid bones, in the throat, were both fractured, and it was determined that the strangulation had been carried out manually.

A description of the dead woman was published in the newspapers, and this led Mary Ann Leat to come forward, and identify the body as that of her sister, forty-eight-year-old Rosina Field. Rosina was the wife of William Edward Field, but had been separated from him for some time, and had since been living at a lodging house at 13 Duncan Terrace, also in Islington.

Meanwhile, Frederick Murphy was absent from his own lodgings, at 57a Colebrooke Row, and a police hunt was launched for him. However, before officers had the chance to find him, Murphy walked into the police station at Poplar, on 15 May, and said he wished to make a statement about the body in the cellar.

In that statement, Murphy claimed that he had gone into the shop on Thursday 13 May, in order to do some cleaning, and in the course of his work, had gone down into the cellar, and found the woman's body. He admitted that he had moved the body, in order to hide it, but denied having anything whatsoever to do with her death. He had, since then, told much the same story to Ethel Marshall, which is why she had agreed to deliver the letter for him on the Friday. However, further inquiries showed that Murphy was not telling the whole truth.

Morris Fieldberry was a builder, and had recently been doing some work at 17 Islington Green. He told the police that at 7.00am, on 12 May, he had seen Murphy, a man he knew well, letting himself into number 22. He had had a woman with him and, although Fieldberry was unable to positive identify the woman, he did remember a very distinctive blue coat, which she had been wearing. Shown the coat that Rosina had been wearing, when her body was discovered, Fieldberry confirmed that it was the one he had seen.

Herbert Robert Fleming had known Murphy for some eighteen months, and also knew Rosina, though he knew her as Rosie. Fleming told the police that on Coronation Day, 12 May, Rosie had borrowed 2d from him, so that she could buy herself a cup of tea at a cafe. Later that same day, just after 8.00pm, he saw Rosie again, and this time she was with Murphy. Two hours later, at 10.00pm, he saw Murphy again, and this time he was alone.

The statements given by those two men, placed the dead woman in Murphy's company throughout 12 May. It must be remembered that Murphy had not only claimed that he knew nothing about Rosina's murder, but claimed that he had not known the woman at all. It was enough to arrest him, and charge him with her murder.

Frederick Murphy appeared at the Old Bailey on 30 June 1937, before the Lord Chief Justice, Lord Hewart. The proceedings lasted until 2 July, during which time the prisoner was defended by Mr F Ashe Lincoln and Mr Michael Peacock. The case for the Crown was led by Mr L A Byrne, who was assisted by Mr Christmas Humphreys.

Witnesses were called who showed that not only had Murphy known the dead woman, but that he had known her for some considerable time. John Donoghue recalled going to the Blue Hall cinema, on Upper Street, on 26 February 1937. As he left the cinema, at around 10.00pm, he noticed a woman, a known prostitute, who had accosted him some days before. She was now with a man, aged around fifty, and five feet six, or seven, inches tall. Donoghue was walking in the same direction as the couple, and eventually saw them stop at a furniture shop at 22 Islington Green. The man looked about the street, and then used a key to open the door. Both he and the woman, then entered the shop. Since that time, Donoghue had positively identified Murphy as the man, and Rosina as the woman.

John William Glover knew Rosina well, and he recalled a meeting with her, in Clerkenwell. Glover, who knew she was a prostitute, asked her how business was, and she replied that there wasn't much about. She went on to say that she wasn't unduly worried, though, as she knew a man, who would let her sleep in a furniture shop, opposite to Collins Music Hall, if she ever ran out of money. The prosecution pointed out that almost directly opposite the music hall, was number 22, Islington Green.

The next witness proved that Murphy was in the habit of using the shop for his own sexual purposes. Emily Robinson, who was a fellow lodger at 13 Duncan Terrace, with Rosina, and who also worked as a prostitute, testified that on 6 May, she had been approached by Murphy, who invited her into number 22, so that they might have sex. She had agreed, and they had performed the deed, on a dirty mattress in the cellar. For her services, Murphy paid her the princely sum of 8d, but also told her to help herself to a rug in the shop.

All this was enough for the jury, who, after a deliberation of forty-five minutes, found Murphy guilty as charged. Only now could a number of interesting facts be revealed. The first, was that Murphy had a long criminal record. No less than five previous offences were listed against his name, and these included convictions for assault, living on immoral earnings, receiving, and theft. Of more relevance, though, was an event in 1929.

On 12 March 1929, a woman's body had been found in Flint Street, Walworth. Catherine Peck had been found with her throat cut, and the police investigation showed that earlier that night, she had been seen drinking in the *Wheatsheaf* public house in Leman Street, with a man named Frederick Murphy. Murphy had been arrested and charged with murder but, at his trial on 28 May, had been found not guilty and discharged. Coincidentally, Catherine Peck's nickname had been Rose.

Murphy entered an appeal against his conviction for the

murder of Rosina Field, and this was heard, on 29 July, by Justices Swift, Finlay and du Parcq. They saw no reason to interfere with either the verdict or the sentence of death, and duly dismissed the application. As Murphy left the courtroom he shouted at the judges: 'I hope you have a good holiday.'

There was no reprieve and, on Tuesday 17 August 1937, Frederick Murphy was hanged at Pentonville, by Alfred Allen and Thomas Phillips.

# Harry Morley
## 1947

Martha Ann Varley was very pleased with her extra present. It was Christmas Eve 1947, and her husband had just given her a cigarette case and a lighter. The only problem was that the lighter did not have any fuel. She would have to get some from the shops.

Taking three penny coins from her purse, Martha asked her eight-year-old son, Ronald James Varley, to run down to Hall's shop at 62 Tollington Way. It was around 6.00pm when Ronald left the house to go on his errand.

The round trip should have only taken Ronald a few minutes, even if the shop were busy, but by 6.30pm, he had still not returned home. Martha was not unduly worried, however. She knew that her two other sons, twelve-year-old Frederick and ten-year-old Henry, had gone to look in a toy shop in Holloway Road. She had no doubt that Ronald had gone to meet up with them. It was, after all, Christmas.

At 6.40pm, Frederick and Henry arrived home to say that had seen nothing of Ronald. The family began to search for the missing boy, even drafting in help from some of the neighbours, but still there was no trace of young Ronald. At 7.00pm, Ronald's parents reported the boy missing at Holloway police station, before returning home to see if Ronald had appeared yet.

A list of all Ronald's friends was made and Frederick and Henry were despatched to the various houses to see if Ronald was at any of them. The search continued, but by the time Mr and Mrs Varley returned home, at 10.20pm, there was still no news of Ronald.

One of the people who had been helping in the search was

George Murphy, Martha's brother-in-law. At 10.20pm, as the Varley's returned home, George updated them as to how the search was going, and said that he did not think there was much more they could do that night. The search party was going to go home, and intended to call in at a pub on the way, for a quick drink. However, before that, George would search the bomb site nearby. He did, after all, have a powerful torch with him. There was an old bombed out shop there, a large area of cleared land, and an old air-raid shelter and George said he would check them all out before he went for his drink.

George Murphy began his search of the site, as he had promised. His wife stood a few steps behind him, checking the shapes outlined in the beam of the torch. Finally, George climbed down into the air-raid shelter. His torch beam played around the debris and suddenly his wife gave out a blood-curdling scream. There, lying on the ground, amongst the rubble, was the body of Ronald Varley.

George's first instinct, quite naturally, was to pick up the child but another of the searchers, Alfred Brindle, alerted by the scream, ran to the scene and advised George to leave everything where it was until the police arrived. There might be valuable forensic evidence, or other clues on the boy's body. George Murphy stepped back and the body remained undisturbed.

The police investigation soon revealed some very interesting information. Sarah Letitia Dean ran Hall's shop, a confectioners and tobacconists, from 62 Tollington Way. She recalled Ronald coming into the shop, at some time between 6.15pm and 6.30pm, and buying two petrol tubes for a lighter. Sarah was absolutely certain that Ronald had paid her with a 6d piece, and received a 3d piece in change. Ronald's mother was equally certain that she had only given him three pennies and that Ronald had no money of his own. Where had he got that 6d piece, and why had it taken him so long to get to the shop? Also, the transaction meant that Ronald should still have had a 3d piece and three 1d pieces, but no money was found on or near his body. He did, however, have the two petrol tubes. One was close to his feet and the other lay near his left hand.

There was also the fact that when his body was found, Ronald's fly-buttons were undone. The boy wore short trousers and his mother confirmed that whenever he needed to urinate, he would do so by lifting his trouser leg up, not by undoing his flys. The suggestion was that the motive for the crime was some sort of sexual attack, though the post-mortem would confirm that Ronald had not been raped, but had been strangled to death.

A potentially important witness had also come forward by this time. Stanley William Harris was twelve years old and lived at 29 Landseer Road. At 6.10pm on 24 December, Stanley, his ten-year- old sister Patsy and his three-year-old brother Jimmy had gone to Hall's shop, to buy some cigarettes for their father. As they passed the bomb shelter, Jimmy fell over some rubble and grazed his leg. As Stanley wiped his brother's leg, with his handkerchief, a man approached them, from the doorway of the shelter. The man asked what had happened and Jimmy started to tell him but, when he looked up, the man had vanished. Jimmy was, however, able to give a description of the man. He was about five feet two inches tall, around sixty years old and had a tear in his trouser leg.

The police investigation continued and part of that was a series of door-to-door enquiries. It was this that led Constable Kitching to knock on the door of a mission hall at 93 Tollington Way. There was no reply, but the dutiful Kitching called at the address repeatedly until, finally, on the afternoon of 26 December, the door was opened by sixty-three-year-old Harry Morley, the caretaker.

Seeing the officer's uniform, Morley immediately said: 'I know nothing about it. It is a terrible business. I never went out. I didn't hear any screams. I never heard a thing. When I came home at quarter past six there were no children about, which is most unusual.'

Morley was asked to give details of his movements on 24 December. He explained that he was actually the caretaker of two mission halls. His main work was at the one situated in Elthorne Road, but he lived at this one in Tollington Way. He explained that he had been carrying out his duties at Elthorne Road and had, as he had explained, arrived home at 6.15pm and not got out again.

Constable Kitching reported all his findings at the police station later that same day and, with each report, included a brief description of any male he had spoken to. Once all the reports were filed, it was seen that the description of Morley, as given by Kitching, was a very close match to the one given by Stanley Harris of the man he had seen in the shelter. It was decided to take a closer look at Harry Morley.

When Constable Kitching returned to 93 Tollington Way, he had with him Detective Inspector Jack Miller and Divisional Detective Inspector Albert Hare. Morley, once again, immediately went onto the defensive. He said he had not spoken to any children at all, but was asked to go to the police station to make a written statement.

It was whilst Morley was waiting to be interviewed that Inspector Miller noticed some fibre flecks on Morley's trousers. When Ronald's body had been discovered, it had been laying close to an old cushion, which had some of the stuffing coming out of it. The fibres on Morley's clothing seemed to be identical to those on the cushion so samples were taken for analysis. Inspector Miller also saw a mark on the shoulder of Morley's jacket. It looked like brick dust, or possibly whitewash and again indicated that he might well have been inside the shelter.

Morley was questioned at length and, after some time, admitted that he had, after all, spoken to some children. He recalled speaking to a boy who had fallen over and later shouted at two boys who were sitting on the edge of a water tank. He still maintained that he had never been into the shelter where Ronald's body was found.

Later still, the story changed again. Now he admitted that he had been in the shelter but only because he had suddenly been overcome with diarrhoea and had to defecate. It was gently pointed out to him that no trace of that had been found in the shelter. Morley thought hard for a few moments then claimed that he had done it in a newspaper, carried it home and flushed it down the toilet.

It was obvious that the police believed none of this. A report, drawn up at the time of these interviews by Inspector Miller, and preserved in The National Archives, at Kew, show that he believed Morley to be, 'garrulous, effeminate, crafty and a typical old sodomite'. It was, of course, long before the advent of political correctness.

After further questioning, Morley admitted that he had been in the shelter with Ronald after all. He claimed that the boy had come to him voluntarily and denied that he had touched him sexually in any way. He ended his admission with: 'I love children,' before making a full statement, in which he admitted giving Ronald a sixpenny piece.

This made an interesting admission. The police knew that Ronald had been to the shop and paid for the petrol with a 6d. Morley must, therefore, have encountered Ronald before he went to Hall's, and then waited for him afterwards and taken him into the shelter, probably for a sexual purpose. Then he had either panicked at what he had done, or the boy had struggled, and Morley had strangled him. As a result, Morley was charged with murder, at 12.30pm on 27 December 1947.

Morley's trial took place in February 1948, before Mr Justice Birkett. The first witness was Stanley Harris who detailed what he had seen on 24 December. Unfortunately for the prosecution, though Stanley was an excellent witness, he could not say with certainty that the man he had seen was the prisoner in the dock.

Terence Fleming was eight years old and lived at 120 Sussex Way. He knew Ronald very well, as they were in the same class at school. On 24 December, Terence had been sent to Hall's shop, to get some cigarettes for his father but, on the way, he had stopped to look into the window of the bicycle shop nearby. As he looked at the gleaming machines he noticed Ronald leaving Hall's shop and heading off in the direction of his house. The two boys waved to each other. Terence believed that this was at about 6.10pm, but he couldn't be sure.

Archibald Burman lived at 64 Tollington Way, but on the evening of 24 December, he had gone to visit his parents at number 95. Whilst he was there his mother asked him to dispose of some old empty milk bottles, and Archibald had put seven or eight into a bag, with the intention of dumping them in the air-raid shelter.

It was around 6.40pm when he approached the shelter, but he saw a man standing at the entrance, so, instead of going in, Archibald dumped the bottles near the bombed out shop. As he did so, the man from the shelter walked past him, heading towards Cornwallis Road. The description Archibald gave did not match Morley. The man he had seen was aged thirty-six to forty, about five eight to five ten and had a long thin face.

There was, however, the fact that Morley had admitted being in the shelter with Ronald. The jury found it impossible to believe that Morley, a known homosexual, had taken a child into the shelter, left him alive and well and then someone else had gone in and killed the child. The verdict, when it came on 12 February, was that Morley was guilty and he was then sentenced to death.

An appeal was entered, and duly dismissed, but Morley did not hang. On 5 April 1948, his defence team received notification from the Home Office that His Majesty had commuted the sentence to one of life imprisonment.

# Chapter 36

# Michael Demetrios Xinaris
# 1955

ineteen-year-old James Frederick Robinson was home on leave from the Army and, on the evening of Friday 18 February 1955, had been out with a couple of his friends. By some time after 10.30pm, the group were in the Blue Kettle cafe, which was situated in an alleyway off Islington High Street.

At around 11.00pm, a group of Teddy boys, dressed in their elaborate uniforms, also entered the cafe. Robinson found this most amusing, and made a few derogatory remarks about the group. One of them, Michael Xinaris, a Cypriot, known to his friends as Nicky, took objection to this and the two men squared up for a fight.

Friends of both men managed to get the intended combatants to sit down again at their respective tables, but the peace was short lived. It was clear that sooner or later, this would escalate into a full fist-fight and so the owner of the establishment, Frank Luigi Lurati, suggested that if they wanted to fight, they should take it outside. The two men, along with various friends, then strolled outside and the sounds of a fight then shattered the quiet night air.

It was only a couple of minutes later that Frank Lurati went outside. To his horror he found that Robinson was now lying on the ground, bleeding profusely from a deep wound in his neck. He had been stabbed and, as Luarto looked up, he saw eighteen-year-old Xinaris running away down the High Street.

The police were called and two officers, Constable John Miles and Constable John Coker, arrived in the alleyway at around 11.30pm. It was Miles who accompanied Robinson in the ambulance that carried him to hospital. Constable Coker stayed at the crime scene and guarded the discarded knife, which lay on the ground close to where Robinson had been lying. Later, he would hand the weapon over to Detective Sergeant Kenneth Percival but, by that time, James Robinson had been delivered to the hospital, where he was pronounced as dead on arrival.

A number of witnesses gave the police the name of Nicky Xinaris, as the man who had inflicted the fatal wound, and he was arrested at his home, 276 City Road, Finsbury, early the following morning, Saturday 19 February. Charged with murder, Xinaris faced his trial on 15 April 1955.

Rudolph Farace was one of Xinaris's friends, and had been with him on the night of the attack upon Robinson. Farace stated that the group had gone to the shopping arcade in the High Street at Islington, and from there decided to go for a coffee in the Blue Kettle. They had sat at a table near the door, whilst Robinson and his friends were sitting near the tea urn, close to the counter. After recounting the details of the argument inside the cafe, Farace confirmed that they had then gone outside into the alleyway, where Robinson struck the first blow, hitting Xinaris in the side of the head on the left side. Farace had then briefly gone back inside the cafe, ostensibly to tell those who had remained at the tables that there was a fight going on. By the time he got back outside, Robinson was standing between numbers 28 and 30 High Street. He had blood coming out of his mouth and neck, as he staggered back into the alleyway and fell. There was no sign of Xinaris at that time.

Robert Ernest Allsop was another of the young men in Xinaris's group. He had heard some sort of remark from Robinson, whereupon Xinaris had stood in front of the table, staring down at him. Robinson had said: 'Who are you looking at?' to which Xinaris had replied: 'Looking at you.' As they then moved towards each other, it was Rudolph Furnace who stood between them and separated them. Then, as they all sat down again at the table, Allsop saw Farace reach into his pocket and hand something to Xinaris.

After Frank Lurati, the cafe proprietor, had given his evidence, the prosecution called Henry George Young. He was a friend of the dead man, and had been with him at the table close to the counter, when the gang of Teddy Boys came in. Also sitting with him and Robinson was James Ingram and, after the initial remarks and the two men squaring up to each other, it had been Young and Ingram who both pulled Robinson back down into his seat. After the fight had taken place outside, Young had seen the knife lying on the ground, and had stood near it so that none of Xinaris's friends could pick it up. When the two constables arrived, Young pointed out the knife and, once the ambulance had arrived, Young also went in the ambulance to the hospital.

Dr Anthony Bashford had attended to the patient as soon as the ambulance arrived at the hospital, but there was nothing he could do for Robinson. He was dead by the time he arrived at 11.45pm.

The post-mortem had been carried out by Professor Cedric Keith Simpson. He reported three stab wounds on Robinson's body. The first was a three-inch-deep and quite long wound on the left hip. The second was a wound on the left arm, but the fatal wound was a five-inch-deep one on the left side of the neck, underneath Robinson's jaw. This wound had severed the carotid artery and opened up Robinson's windpipe. Robinson had lost a great deal of blood, especially from that last wound, and that haemorrhage was the direct cause of death.

There could be no doubt that Xinaris was responsible for Robinson's death and the jury only deliberated for a short time, before returning their guilty verdict, though they did add a recommendation to mercy. Only now could it be revealed that just two months before the attack upon James Robinson, Xinaris had been arrested for carrying a knife, and had been warned as to his future behaviour by the magistrates. There could, of course, now only be one sentence for the murder and, having donned the black cap, the judge duly sentenced Nicky Xinaris to death by hanging.

An appeal was entered and heard on 25 May, before Justices Hilbery, Gorman and Havers. They saw no reason to interfere with either the verdict, or the sentence and the appeal was dismissed.

Michael Xinaris did not, however, pay the ultimate penalty for his crime. No doubt due to the fact that he was so young, the sentence was commuted to one of life imprisonment.

Records preserved at The National Archives at Kew show that the authorities wished, in fact, to add to that punishment. It was suggested that once he had served his sentence, Xinaris should be deported to his native Cyprus. After much debate, and a number of letters being exchanged, the powers that be eventually ruled that since Xinaris had lived in England since he was a baby, he had no real links with Cyprus and so could not be thrown out of the country.

Michael Xinaris only served some eight and a half years in prison. He was released on licence on 18 October 1963.

# Chapter 37

# Ronald Henry Marwood
# 1959

At 10.30pm, on the night of Sunday 14 December 1958, Constable Raymond Henry Summers was on his beat, at the corner of Seven Sisters Road and Isledon Road. He was walking towards Holloway Road, when he saw what looked like a massive street fight.

A large group of youths, perhaps thirty strong or more, were milling about on the pavement outside Grey's Dancing Academy, at 133 Seven Sisters Road. Bravely, Summers went to investigate and, seeing him approach, many of the youths ran off. However, by the time he arrived at the scene, there were still perhaps a dozen men standing around.

Tempers were running high, and it was clear that in order to nip the problem in the bud, Summers would have to move people on. Again not seeking to take the easy way out of this situation, Constable Summers approached one of the tallest and biggest men there: Michael David Bloom, a man aged twenty-four and standing six feet three inches tall. Words were exchanged, and Summers decided that he would have to arrest Bloom. The two men struggled for a few moments, but eventually Summers managed to grab hold of one of Bloom's arms and pin it up behind his back. The officer then began to walk Bloom away from the scene, when another member of the group, Ronald Henry Marwood, stepped forward and appeared to strike the Constable in his back.

In fact, Marwood had had a knife in his hand and Summers had now been stabbed. In great pain and losing a good deal of blood, Summers had no choice but to release his grip on Bloom, and watch as the two young men, and their friends, ran off in different directions. Constable Summers managed to stagger off down the street and, in all, hobbled a total of forty-three yards before he collapsed outside the Co-operative store, further down Seven Sisters Road.

Frederick Francis McLoughlin and Edward Walter Hassall had both been walking down Seven Sisters Road, and had seen part of the attack on Constable Summers. They had also seen the men run off, and Summers staggering along the road. They, of course, had no idea at this stage that Summers had been stabbed but, once he fell, they ran forward to see what help they could offer. A passing car, driven by Kenneth Edward Hudd, was stopped. There was a telephone box close by and Hudd immediately rang for the police, but it was obvious that the officer had been badly hurt and needed urgent medical attention. Rather than wait for an ambulance, McLoughlin, Hassall and Hudd all helped to gently place Summers in Hudd's car, and they then drove the stricken officer to the Royal Northern Hospital in Holloway Road. It was all to no avail. Constable Summers was dead by the time the three samaritans managed to get him to the hospital.

Various witnesses had seen something of the fracas in the street, and they were able to supply descriptions of many of those involved. Those descriptions, and other evidence led to the arrest of eleven men, all of whom were charged with affray. In addition to Michael Bloom, the police also arrested Brian Robert Murray, George William Fletcher, Frederick John Jackman and his brother, Ronald James Jackman, Brian John Thwaites, John Budd, Ronald Bergonzi, Frederick Robert Newbolt, David Henry Bailey and Peter Sydney Dean. All would eventually appear in court on 11 February 1959 but, in the meantime, there was no sign of the man who had stabbed Constable Summers: Ronald Henry Marwood. He had simply vanished from his home at 37 Huntingdon Street.

Although none of the men who had been with Marwood would confirm that he had struck the fatal blow with his knife, they did reveal some of their movements on the night that Summers died. Exactly one year before, on 14 December 1957, Marwood had married, so the night of the stabbing was his first wedding anniversary.

Marwood had, apparently, asked his wife to go out with him to celebrate, but she had decided to stay at home. She had had no objection, however, to her husband going out with his friends. Marwood had first gone to the *Spanish Patriot* public house in White Conduit Street. From there he and his friends had gone to the *Double R Club*, in Bow Road, where they had remained until closing time. In all, it was estimated that Marwood had consumed around ten pints of beer in those two establishments.

Once the *Double R* had closed, the group decided to go to Barries Dance Academy at 12 Highbury Corner, and it was from there that they walked to Grey's Dancing Academy. One of their number went to the front door, and almost immediately, another gang of youths dashed out and a street fight started. Coshes, choppers and knives were used, and some minor injuries inflicted, before Constable Summers had appeared, and many of the youths ran off.

In fact, it soon became clear that two officers had actually interviewed Marwood after the fight. Once news of Constable Summers stabbing had been broadcast on the police radios, officers went in search of the men who had been fighting in Seven Sisters Road. At 11.00pm, two officers in a police van, Constable Sidney Robert Baker and Constable Cyril Burt, had seen four men walking down Hornsey Road. As the police van approached them, two of the men ran off but the other two were stopped and questioned.

The two men identified themselves as Marwood and David Henry Bailey, and even as the two officers spoke to them, they could not help but notice that Marwood had a deep cut across the fingers on his right hand. Asked to explain their movements that night, Marwood lied, and said that they had been drinking at the *Finsbury Park Hotel* and had been involved in a fight there.

Baker and Burt were not prepared to accept this statement at face value. Marwood and Bailey were placed into the police van, and taken to Holloway police station. Both were interviewed separately, and made written statements, which roughly corresponded. At 9.30am the following morning, Monday 15 December, the two men were taken to the *Finsbury Park Hotel* to see if the landlord could confirm their story. Unfortunately, the previous night had been a very busy one and even though Marwood and Bailey indicated where they had been sitting, the landlord said he couldn't possibly remember every customer he had served on the Sunday. As for the supposed fight outside, well, there were constant fights over every weekend and it was likely that there had been one on that weekend too. At this point, since the stories seemed to be acceptable, the two men were driven to their respective homes and released from custody.

Once things in Seven Sisters Road had become clearer, the police decided to interview Marwood and Bailey again. On the morning of Tuesday 16 December, Bailey was taken back into custody and interviewed again. At 7.30pm that evening he finally admitted that he, Marwood and others had been at the scene of Constable Summer's stabbing and that Marwood had probably been the one who used the knife. Of course, by this time, Marwood had left home, and his family claimed to have no idea where he was. They also said that they believed he would not have had anything to do with the stabbing.

On Wednesday 17 December, Marwood's wife, Rosalie, received a letter from her husband, postmarked South Kensington. In that letter he wrote that he could not understand why the police were looking for him, as he had already told them everything he knew when he had been picked up. That letter was handed over to the investigating officers that same day.

On Friday 19 December, as part of the round-up of those who had been involved in the fight, Michael Bloom was arrested. He now confirmed that Constable Summers had arrested him and had his arm pinned behind his back, when Marwood appeared to punch the officer in the back. Summers then let Bloom go and the two men ran off. They then hid in a private garden at 32 Isledon Road and, as they crouched down, Marwood said that he had done the copper. He then showed Bloom the knife before hiding it amongst a pile of garden rubbish. When officers went to that address later that same day, they recovered a bloodstained knife which proved to be the weapon that had been used on Constable Summers.

Still there was no sign of Marwood. On 3 January 1959, his description and a photograph of the wanted man was released to the press. It brought no new leads. By now the police were convinced that Marwood's family knew far more than they were saying so, on 22 January, Rosalie Marwood was interviewed again. She told officers that she believed her husband was being hidden by John Nash, of 41 Macclesfield Road, and Robert Stokes, of 13 Moira Street, off the City Road. Both men were well known to the police but, when they were interviewed, both said that had nothing to do with hiding the wanted man.

Rosalie Marwood had, in fact, given the police one more very important piece of information. Now, finally, she admitted that before he had left home to go into hiding, her husband had admitted to her that he had stabbed a policeman.

Marwood knew that it was only a matter of time before he was picked up. In the event, he saved them the trouble. At 7.30pm, on 27 January 1959, three men walked into the police station on Caledonian Road. The three were Marwood, his uncle, Harry William Day, and his cousin by marriage, Daniel John Carr. Day and Carr both denied that they had been hiding Marwood. He had merely called them, said he wished to give himself up, and had asked them to accompany him to the station.

Taken in for interview Marwood said: 'You can write it all down. I did stab the copper that night. I'll never know why I did it. I have been puzzling over in my mind during the last few weeks why I did it, but there seems no answer.'

Marwood's trial took place at the Old Bailey on 19 March 1959, before Mr Justice Gorman. The prisoner was defended by Mr Neil Lawson and Mr M Levene whilst the prosecution case was outlined by Mr Christmas Humphreys and Mr EJP Cussen.

The law relating to capital punishment had changed in 1957, and now there were just five circumstances in which a case of murder could result in a death sentence. One of those circumstances was the murder of a police officer, or a prison officer, in the course of their duty. That meant that if Marwood were found guilty of the murder of Constable Summers, he would face death by hanging.

In addition to the testimony of the witnesses already mentioned, the prosecution called Dr Francis Camps, who had performed the post-mortem on the dead officer. He reported a single stab wound on the left side of the back, some five inches below shoulder level and some four inches from the midline of the back. The wound had passed into the chest cavity between the sixth and seventh ribs, which was only possible if Constable Summers had had his arm raised at the time the wound was inflicted. The wound had then passed through the upper part of the lower lobe of the left lung and then on into the aorta. The cause of death was loss of blood.

This was an important piece of testimony, for the defence as well as the prosecution. Marwood admitted that he was responsible for Summer's death, but claimed that he had acted in self-defence and so was only guilty of manslaughter. He claimed that he had seen his friend, Bloom, arrested and went to intervene. Constable Summers had told him to step away and pushed him to emphasise the point. Marwood took a step back towards the officer, who then raised his hand. Marwood thought he was going to be attacked. and lashed out in self-defence, not realising that he had the knife in his hand. However, this did not explain how Constable Summers had suffered a wound in his back.

Having considered all the evidence, the jury found Marwood guilty of the capital crime and he was duly sentenced to death. An appeal was heard, in April, and dismissed, but other efforts were made to save Marwood's life. One hundred and fifty members of parliament, mostly Labour, signed an appeal for Marwood to be reprieved. There was also a public petition for mercy, which attracted thousands of signatures. A last minute request to the Attorney General was made for permission to appeal to the House of Lords, but that was rejected for the somewhat irrational excuse that it was out of time. Such a request was supposed to be made within seven days of the death sentence being given. The authorities were not to be moved, just because a man's life was at stake.

On Thursday 7 May 1959, a crowd of more than one thousand

people demonstrated outside the gates of Pentonville prison. At the same time, a group of prisoners inside the jail organised their own demonstration. None of it was to save Marwood from the gallows.

The following day, Friday 8 May, twenty-five-year-old Ronald Henry Marwood, an only child, was hanged by Harry Allen, who was assisted by Harry Robinson.

# Chapter 38

# John Patrick Quinlan
# 1962

There were a number of people living at 125 Andover Road in 1962. The owner of the house was Mary Kate Davitt, but she rented out a couple of rooms to lodgers. Peter Francis Clifford lived in one room and the one next door to his was shared by fifty-one-year-old John Patrick Quinlan and fifteen-year-old Michael Joseph Teahan.

On Monday 16 April, Quinlan, who was employed by London Transport, went to work at 6.20am. He was on duty until 4.30pm but did not go straight home. Instead he went to the company canteen first, had some tea, and finally left at around 4.45pm. From there he walked to Euston Square, where he went to the cinema, leaving there at 8.00pm. He would later claim that after leaving the picture house, he met a prostitute who offered him sex for 10s but he managed to negotiate a reduction to 5s. After that encounter he went to a public house, where he drank just one pint. He then went back to his room at Andover Road, stopping off for fish and chips on the way.

It was around 9.30pm by the time Quinlan arrived home. He sat down and started a letter to a friend of his in the United States, and whilst he was writing it, Michael Teahan arrived home. The two chatted for a while before both went to their respective beds.

At some time during the small hours of the next morning, Quinlan awoke to find that his bed and his pyjamas were wet. He felt disorientated and had something of a headache, but managed to get back to sleep. The next morning, he only woke at 10.00am, but still felt very tired indeed. Glancing across the room, he saw that Michael was also still in bed. That was most unusual as Michael was normally an early riser. Quinlan still didn't feel very well, so decided to stay in bed. At 10.30am he shouted across to Michael, asking him if he was all right. There was no reply.

It was not until noon, when the landlady, Mary Davitt, came into the room, that Quinlan finally got out of bed. Mary was also most surprised to see that Michael was still in bed, and noticed that he looked rather pale. She went over to his bed and saw that he had apparently been sick in the night, as there was some vomit close to his mouth. She tried to rouse him. At one stage she even gently slapped his face, but it was no use. Michael could not answer his landlady, for he was dead.

Dr David Cline attended the scene and confirmed that Michael was dead. He noted that, once the bedclothes were removed, Michael's skin had a pale pinkish tinge. That, added to the fact that he had vomited, and that his room-mate had been feeling sick during the night, led Dr Cline to suggest that Michael had been the victim of an accidental carbon monoxide poisoning, most probably from a faulty gas meter. However, Dr Cline also noted that Michael's body lay in a rather posed position, as if he had been placed in that bed by some other person.

It was 5.15pm on Tuesday 17 April, when Dr Hugh Robert Molesworth Johnson, a forensic pathologist, made his own examination of the young man. He began by noting the frothy vomit that had issued from the corner of Michael's mouth, and the pale cherry pink tinge to his skin. This seemed to confirm that death was due to carbon monoxide poisoning, and Dr Johnson placed the time of death between 1.00am and 5.00am. There was, however, one other factor, which led to police involvement. A good deal of spermatozoa was discovered on Michael's body, and in his anal passage. It seemed that Michael had engaged in anal intercourse some time before he had died. Since there was only one other person in his room, the most likely suspect for that was John Quinlan.

Quinlan had already made a statement to the police, in which he had outlined his movements of the previous night, but had omitted his encounter with the prostitute, and the fact that he had had sex with her. On 18 April, Detective Inspector Thomas

O' Shea called back at Andover Road, to interview Quinlan again. He was not at home, so the officer waited in the street outside. At 11.15pm, he saw Quinlan staggering up the road, obviously the worse for drink. He identified himself as a police officer and told Quinlan that he would be taken to Holloway police station for further questioning. It was there that he made a second statement, now mentioning the prostitute, thus causing the police to conclude that he had deliberately lied the first time he had been interviewed. These factors led to John Quinlan being charged with buggery on 20 April and murder on 9 May.

Quinlan's trial began on 19 June 1962 and would last until 22 June. The prosecution began by explaining that the prisoner had been born on 5 March 1911, in Eire, and was one of a family of twelve children. He had six sisters and five brothers, and had worked for London Transport for the past five years.

William Peter Roxborough told the court that the dead man had been his brother-in-law and would have been sixteen on 25 April 1962. It was Michael's custom to have his evening meal at Roxborough's house. He had done so on the night of 16 April, and had left to go home at 10.05pm. It was a twenty-minute walk, or so, to Michael's lodgings so he would have arrived there shortly before 10.30pm.

The suggestion, by the defence, was that this had been an accidental death, due to a faulty gas meter. No fewer than three men were called to give evidence on the meter in the premises.

Arthur William Lightfoot was a gas-fitter, working for the North Thames Gas Board, and he had fitted a new coin-operated meter at 125 Andover Road at 7.35am on 12 April, just a few days before Michael died. He had tested it at the time and found it to be in perfect working order.

On 17 April, after the tragedy had taken place, the meter was checked by another fitter, Samuel Albert Bateman. He noted that the main stop-cock was in the off position and the lever had been incorrectly placed, so that it was pointing downwards instead of upwards, though this would not render the meter dangerous in any way. Finally, the meter had been checked by Godfrey Gibbs, the District Service manager for the gas board, and he had found it in good order.

Some of this testimony appeared to be negated by the experience of Peter Clifford, who lodged in the room next to the one where Michael had died. He said that he had arrived home at 11.20pm on the night of 16 April, and decided to make himself a cup of tea. He turned the gas on, but found that it must have run out, so placed a shilling in the new meter. Still there was no gas so he gave up on his tea and went to bed.

During the night he heard a loud noise as if someone had fallen. He heard someone moving about outside his room, but did not go to investigate, thinking it was most probably one of the tenants coming home late. The following morning, Peter had a very bad headache, felt sick and had a funny taste in his mouth.

The post-mortem on Michael had been carried out by Dr Francis Edward Camps. He described Michael as being five feet six inches tall and said he had been well nourished in life. There were no signs of external violence on his body but his anal passage was relaxed and there was evidence that there had been anal intercourse on several occasions in the past. In Dr Camps' opinion. Michael had last engaged in anal sex within an hour of his death. Finally, he was able to report that carbon monoxide had been the cause of death and Michael had a 74% saturation in his blood.

Bryan John Culliford was a Senior Scientific Officer at the Forensic Science Laboratory at New Scotland Yard. He reported that both Quinlan and Michael had type-O blood. Quinlan, however, was a secretor, meaning that blood cells were secreted in other bodily fluids such as spittle and sperm.

Mr Culliford had taken an anal swab from Michael's body and had found human spermatozoa in the passageway. The blanket he had slept under also bore semen stains, as did his trousers, pyjama top, vest and underpants. All these stains had been deposited by someone who was not a secretor, showing that they did not belong to Quinlan. There were, however, stains from a group-O secretor on the eiderdown.

The jury retired to debate the case and came to the conclusion that this was clearly an accident. Michael Teahan had obviously inhaled household gas, but Quinlan and Peter Clifford had also been ill that night. It was clear that, despite what the three witnesses from the gas board had said, there was something wrong with the new meter. Coins had been placed in it but, apparently, still no gas was produced. Forensic tests had also shown that if gas was allowed to flow freely inside the house, there was a strong concentrated build up close to Michael's bed. The jury duly returned a not guilty verdict.

A number of questions were never actually answered. Had the gas meter been faulty after all? Should the Gas Board have been called to account for the death of Michael Teahan and, finally, who had Michael had sex with in the hours before his death?

# Chapter 39

# Panayotis Gregoriou
# 1962

Sofronis Theodulou, a Greek Cypriot, ran his cafe from 162 Seven Sisters Road. His clientele consisted largely of other Greeks, one of whom was Costas Vassiliou.

At some time between 6.30pm and 7.00pm on 8 August 1962, Costas parked his car close to the cafe and went inside. He was talking happily to Sofronis when he heard voices outside. Looking through the window he saw two other Greeks talking on the pavement: Panayotis Gregoriou and Demetris Michael, who worked at the nearby barber's shop. There was, however, a problem, for Gregoriou was leaning on Costas' car.

Going outside, Costas said, quite calmly: 'Don't lean on the car.' Gregoriou replied: 'What are you saying? I was not leaning on the car.' Costas simply said: 'You were,' but then emphasised his point by slapping Gregoriou in the face two or three times.

A fist-fight broke out instantly, with Gregoriou throwing the first punch. Sofronis immediately stepped outside and separated the two young men, pulling Costas over to some railings at the side of his cafe. Gregoriou, meanwhile, had gone into the tobacconist's and confectioner's shop next door but, within three or four minutes he was back outside and this time, he had a gun in his hand, a semi-automatic.

Sofronis was standing with his back to his cafe. In front of him, and facing him, was Costas, who was still being berated by Sofronis for fighting in the street. As a result, neither man saw Gregoriou raise the gun and start to fire.

Witnesses would differ over just how many shots were fired. What is beyond doubt is that Costas fell to the ground, dead, and Sofronis was hit twice, though he was not badly injured. Gregoriou, meanwhile, had simply turned on his heel and run off towards Medina Road.

Constable Peter Allen and Constable Ronald Westbury were on routine traffic patrol, when they received a message to go to Seven Sisters Road. Going directly to the scene, they pulled up outside number 162 to find a man lying face up on the pavement, not far from the kerb. As they waited for further help, and medical assistance, Constable Allen made a careful search of the surrounding area, finding four spent shell cases. His colleague, Westbury, marked the area where the body lay in yellow chalk. The ambulance arrived soon afterwards and rushed Costas to the Royal Northern Hospital, where, at 8.00pm, he was seen by Dr Joseph Schember Wismayer, who confirmed that he was dead.

Many of the witnesses to the shooting knew Gregoriou, so the police already knew who they were looking for. They were also given his home address of 8 Bryantwood Road, Drayton Park. They believed that, sooner or later, the wanted man would return home, so two officers, Constable Robert Webster and Constable Banner were sent to wait outside the house. As extra back-up, the two officers had taken Yorick, a rather large police dog, with them.

At midnight, a man fitting the description of Gregoriou was seen walking along, past the tube station. The two officers followed, with Yorick straining at his leash. Once they were sure that this was Gregoriou, the officers stopped him, close to the Express Dairy building, and informed him that he was being arrested and taken to the police station at Holloway.

At the police station, a Greek interpreter, Mr Ferid, was provided, so that Gregoriou would be fully aware of what was taking place. Even before the interview started, Gregoriou exclaimed: 'I am a small man. He hit me and I shot him.'

Later, he made a full written statement. It began:

> I was at the place where the crime took place. A car was standing there, still. A man whom I know and who is a painter, came and stood about six or seven yards away from me. He turned towards me and said: 'Do not bend yourself on the car [sic]. Then he came near me, got hold of me from my jacket and started hitting me.
>
> Sofronis, who is my relative, and who has the coffee shop there, came near us in order to separate us, but the painter continued hitting me. I show you my shin where he kicked me. Sofronis went away without separating us.
>
> I looked on the ground to see if there was anything as [sic] stone or stick which I could get hold of and hit him back. I saw a gun on the ground. I took it and I fired repeatedly. Then I ran away and I threw the pistol in the grass, where I showed to the police.

This statement held two problems for the police. In the first place, the idea that Gregoriou had looked down and found a gun simply lying on the pavement, was a nonsense. They were sure that he had carried that weapon to the scene and taken it out of his pocket inside the tobacconist's shop. The second concern was that the weapon had not been found. It was true that Gregoriou had pointed out a patch of grass, close to the Labour Exchange in Medina Road but, despite a meticulous search, no gun had been found there or anywhere nearby.

Having made his statement, Panayotis Gregoriou was charged with murder but there was one factor that made this case rather different. As we have already seen, in the late 1950s, the law on capital punishment had been amended, so that now only five classes of murder carried a possible death sentence. One of those circumstances was murder, by the use of a firearm. If Gregoriou were found guilty of murder, he would face execution.

Panayotis Gregoriou had been born on 9 February 1934, and had first come to England on 5 April 1961. He began working for a carburettor manufacturer at 223 Marylebone Road, at a wage of £10 10s per week, but had left there on 8 November 1961, after a minor dispute with his supervisor. For some time after that, he had worked as a kitchen porter, at a restaurant at the *Elephant and Castle*, at a reduced salary of £8 a week. For the last few months, he had worked for a doll-maker in Holloway. More important, however, was his mental make-up.

Tests had shown that Gregoriou was of very low intelligence. Asked to name the prime minister, he was unable to do so. The question: 'What is four plus four?' was met with a blank and incredulous stare and when asked to simply repeat the digits three, six, eight, he replied: 'Three, six and a lot of numbers.' He was also unable to tell anyone who he worked for, or where their offices were situated. This, added to his tendency to be highly strung and volatile, would form the basis of his defence in court.

On 1 September 1962, Gregoriou faced his capital murder charge at the Old Bailey. Mr Mervyn Griffith-Jones and Mr SA Norton prosecuted whilst the prisoner was defended by Mr A P Antoniades. Another interpreter, Mr Hassam Enver, was provided, so that Gregoriou could understand all the testimony.

Demetris Michael had stepped outside of the barber's shop, where he worked, a few minutes before the shooting took place. After having a brief conversation with Gregoriou, he had seen Costas come out of the cafe and remonstrate with the prisoner for leaning on his car. Demetris had stepped inside the sweet shop and stayed there, once he heard the sound of gunfire.

Sofronis Theodulou, the owner of the cafe, said that after the first couple of shots were fired, Costas fell forward into his arms. As he slipped down to the pavement, Gregoriou carried on firing. Two of those shots hit him; one in his hand, the other in his right thigh. He was taken to the Royal Northern Hospital in the same ambulance as Costas.

Jack Shaw owned the shop next door. He had seen the

altercation between the two men, and Sofronis attempt to separate them. He too had gone out, briefly, to tell them to go away and fight somewhere else. After hearing the shooting, it was Shaw who telephoned for an ambulance and the police.

George Constantinou had been to the Astoria cinema in Finsbury Park with two friends of his, Christopher Constantinou, who was no relation, and Evangelos Michael. They walked past the scene of the shooting, but were on the opposite side of the road. Having past the shops they heard raised voices, stopped and turned around to see what was happening. George believed that five or six shots were fired and saw Gregoriou run away afterwards. Some elderly man put his foot out to try to trip Gregoriou, but when he pointed the gun at him, the man let him pass.

Another passer-by was sixteen-year-old Harold Witts, who was riding his bicycle down Seven Sisters Road, when he heard the two men arguing. He stopped a little further on and watched, thinking he would see a good fist fight. Instead he saw Gregoriou come out of the sweet shop, put his hand under his jacket and bring out a gun.

The post-mortem on Costas was carried out by Dr Francis Edward Camps on 9 August. He counted a large number of entrance and exit wounds on the body, including wounds on the right knee, the right hand, the back of the right forearm, the right buttock and a cluster of wounds in the back. In all he estimated that at least seven and possibly as many as nine bullets had been fired.

The matter was now for the jury to decide. There could be no doubt that Gregoriou had brought the gun with him to Seven Sisters Road, and used it once Costas had struck him. However, they also took into account his highly-strung personality and low intelligence, and came to the conclusion that he was not totally responsible for his actions. Bearing that in mind they found Gregoriou not guilty of murder, but guilty of manslaughter. He was then sentenced to life imprisonment.

# Chapter 40

# Kenneth Halliwell
# 1967

I n 1951, two young men, both aspiring actors, met at the Royal Academy of Dramatic Arts, in London. They had come from widely differing backgrounds.

The youngest of the two men was eighteen-year-old John Kingsley Orton, a man who had been born in Leicester on 1 January 1933. He had not excelled academically at school, and had failed his eleven plus examination. He had, nevertheless, worked hard and, finally, gained a scholarship to RADA. The elder of the two, was twenty-five-year-old Kenneth Halliwell.

Halliwell had not had the most auspicious of upbringings. Largely ignored by his father, he had been perhaps over protected by his mother. When Halliwell was just eleven years of age, his mother had been stung, inside her mouth, by a wasp and, highly allergic to its venom, she had tragically died.

At about the same time, Halliwell had managed to win a scholarship, to the Wirral Grammar School, where he became a classic scholar, passing his Higher School Certificates in 1943. At this time, the Second World War was still raging and, upon leaving school, Halliwell was called up to serve in the forces. He registered as a conscientious objector and was, consequently, sent down the coal mines. In 1946, after his service was over, he returned to Birkenhead where, three years later, in 1949, his father committed suicide by gassing himself. Soon after this, Halliwell moved down to London, and entered RADA.

Halliwell and Orton soon became close friends and, since both were homosexual, they also became lovers, at a time when such relationships were still illegal. After leaving RADA, both tried, without success, to earn a living as actors but, also turned their hands to writing. The two men wrote a number of novels together, none of which were published and, if anything, Halliwell, with the better education, acted as a tutor for his younger partner, as they lived together at 25 Noel Road, Islington.

For a time, success eluded both men. At one stage they amused themselves by stealing and defacing books from Islington library. Caught in September 1962, they were arrested and charged with theft and damaging property. Found guilty of those offences, they received the rather Draconian sentence of six months' imprisonment, and a fine. Orton served his sentence at Eastchurch, in Kent, whilst Halliwell was sent to Ford prison, in Sussex.

Almost as soon as they were released from prison, Orton, now using the name Joe Orton, had a radio play, *The Ruffian on the Stair*, accepted by the BBC. This was in 1963, and the following year, his first stage-play, *Entertaining Mr Sloane*, opened, on 6 May, to much critical acclaim. This was followed, in 1965, by a second, even more successful play, *Loot*, which premiered on 27 September 1966, and won the Evening Standard Drama Award, for the best play that year. The roles between the two lovers had now changed dramatically.

Halliwell, the more educated, was now overshadowed by Orton. He was unable to cope with being sidelined, and began to suffer from bouts of acute depression. He was prescribed tablets for that depression, and also to aid him sleep. Meanwhile, Joe Orton was penning yet another play, *What the Butler Saw*, which would surely bring him more fame and reward. Things were coming to an inevitable conclusion.

On 5 August 1967, Orton met a friend, Peter Nolan, in the *Chelsea Potter* public house on the King's Road. They talked about a number of things, but at one stage Orton said that he had found himself another boyfriend, and wished to end his relationship with Halliwell, though he wasn't sure how to go about it.

Meanwhile, Halliwell's doctor was becoming increasingly concerned about his mental state, and had advised him to seek professional help, from a psychiatrist. They spoke, on the telephone, at 10.00pm on Wednesday 9 August, when the doctor rang to give Halliwell the psychiatrist's address. Halliwell commented: 'Don't worry, I'm feeling better now. I'll go and see the doctor tomorrow morning.'

On the morning of Thursday 10 August 1967, Orton had an appointment to discuss a film script, *Up Against It,* which he was writing for The Beatles. A chauffeur-driven car pulled up to the flat in Noel Road, but there was no reply when the driver rang the bell. The police were called, the door forced open, and the two men were found inside; both of them were dead.

At some time the previous night, 9 August, Halliwell had taken a hammer and rained nine blows onto Orton's head. He had then written a short note, before taking an overdose of twenty-two Nembutal tablets. In fact, the subsequent medical examination, was to show that Halliwell had actually died first.

The short note left by Halliwell read: 'If you read his diary, all will be explained K.H.' There was also a postscript: 'Especially the latter part.' When Orton's diary was found, there were many references to other sexual encounters, which he had had, including many in public toilets. Halliwell, it seemed, had not only been unable to cope with his partner's glittering success, but had also been depressed by his other affairs.

# Chapter 41

# Other Crimes
# post-1900

## (1) Amelia Sach and Annie Walters, 1903

For some years, Amelia Sach had run a home for unmarried mothers, in East Finchley. For a financial consideration, she would attend to young ladies through their confinement and, usually for a larger fee, she would find homes for the babies afterwards. Occasionally, however, it might prove difficult to find a suitable home, and that was when Amelia called on the services of her friend, fifty-four-year old Annie Walters.

Annie had a tried and tested method of dealing with unwanted children. She would administer a few drops of chlorodyne, a morphine-based sedative, and in due course, the babies would die from asphyxia. On the rare occasions that this failed to work, Annie would help things along by smothering the child.

In August 1903, a lady named Galley, one of the inmates at the home, gave birth to a healthy baby boy. Amelia informed her that she had a suitable home ready, and the fee would be £30, a considerable sum in 1903 (worth about £1,700 today).

In the meantime, the police had been alerted to the somewhat strange behaviour of Annie Walters, and the fact that a large number of children seemed to be passing through her hands. So, when she left her Islington home, on 18 November 1902, she was followed by a police officer. Stopped at South Kensington station, Annie was found to have in her possesion the dead body of Miss Galley's child.

Annie and Amelia were both arrested, and appeared at the Old Bailey, before Mr Justice Darling, on 15 January 1903. The trial lasted for two days, at the end of which both women were found guilty of murder and sentenced to death.

On Tuesday 3 February 1903, Sach and Walters were hanged together at Holloway prison, by William Billington and Henry Pierrepoint. It was the only occasion in the twentieth century where two women were hanged together.

## (2) Frederick Gardner, 1905

On Saturday 7 October 1905, Frederick Gardner was enjoying a quiet drink, at the *Green Man* public house, in Green Man's Lane, when a group of men approached him, and half jokingly asked if he was going to treat them to a drink. When Gardner refused, he was attacked and beaten by the men, who then ran off. Gardner picked himself up, wiped the blood from his nose, and went looking for the men who had assaulted him.

Gardner went to various pubs, including the *George The Fourth* and *The Golden Fleece*, but it was not until he returned to the *Green Man* that he found one of them, Benjamin William Crow.

Crow immediately asked Gardner if he were going to hit him, and Gardner said no, pointing out that he had a bad hand, but before he had even finished speaking, Crow lashed out, and struck him in the face. To defend himself, Gardner then struck Crow on the jaw. Crow fell back, struck his head on the edge of the pavement, never recovered consciousness, and was dead within a few hours. Gardner, meanwhile, not realising the extent of his opponent's injuries, had simply gone home.

Charged with manslaughter, Gardner appeared in court on 13 November. The first witness, Sergeant James Smith, pointed out that Gardner had handed himself into the police station, on 8 October, and had announced: 'My name is Frederick Gardner. I had a fight with Crow. I hear he is dead. I struck the man. I did not mean to kill him; it was a drunken quarrel.'

Dr George Madden testified that Crow had suffered from a fractured skull, and corresponding compression of the brain. The injury could easily have been caused by either a severe blow, or by Crow's head coming into contact with the pavement, or kerb.

Edwin Louis Berry had seen the brief altercation between the two men, and testified that the blow, which Gardner had inflicted upon Crow, was nothing more than an ordinary punch to the left of the jaw. Crow had staggered backwards, fallen and his head hit the kerb with a terrible smash.

The jury considered the evidence and decided that Gardner had acted in self-defence and returned a not guilty verdict.

### (3) Frederick Henry Seddon, 1912

When Frank Ernest Vonderache called at 63 Tollington Park, Islington, to see his cousin, Eliza Barrow, who lodged there, he was shocked to find that she had died, on Thursday 14 September 1911, and was now buried. What was even more of a shock, was that Miss Barrow had apparently signed all of her property and assets to her landlord, Frederick Henry Seddon.

Frank Vonderache believed that this was totally out of character for his cousin, and this, added to the haste in which she had been buried, led him to take his concerns to the police.

Police investigations showed that Miss Barrow had first fallen ill on 1 September 1911, and the doctor had attended a number of times before she died, two weeks later. The cause of death had been given as acute enteritis, but by this time, the police had come to think that her death was just too convenient for Frederick Seddon. The previous year, Miss Barrow had signed over some property, and some stocks, in return for an annuity of a few pounds. Now that she was dead, all the property belonged to Seddon, and he had paid out very little in return. It was decided to exhume Miss Barrow's body and subject it to a second post-mortem.

The exhumation took place on 15 November, and Bernard Spilsbury performed the new examination. He determined that the true cause of death was arsenic poisoning. Both Seddon, and his wife, Margaret Ann, were arrested and charged with murder.

The trial of the husband and wife opened on 4 March 1912, and lasted until 14 March. At the end of that time, the jury found Mrs Seddon not guilty, but determined that Frederick was guilty as charged. Mr Justice Bucknill then sentenced him to death.

A subsequent appeal having failed, Henry Seddon was hanged, at Pentonville, on Thursday 18 April 1912, by John Ellis and Thomas Pierrepoint. Right up to the end, Seddon claimed that he was innocent of any involvement in the death of Eliza Barrow.

### (4) Joe Meek, 1967

Born Robert George Meek, on 5 April 1929, Meek became a famous record producer and songwriter, based at his studios at 304 Holloway Road, Islington. Amongst his most memorable productions was *Telstar*, the first record by a British group, the Tornados, ever to reach number one in the United States, and *Have I The Right*, by the Honeycombs.

Unfortunately, the early success soon ended and Meek fell into debt, causing him acute depression. Allied to that, was the fact that Meek was a homosexual, at a time when this was still illegal in Britain, and punishable by imprisonment.

Things came to a head in January 1967 when police in Tattingstone, Suffolk, found the body of Bernard Oliver, a rent-boy, dumped in a suitcase. As part of their investigation, officers said that they intended to interview all known homosexuals within the City and, since Meek had a previous association with Oliver, he suspected that he would figure heavily in those interviews.

Just a few days later, on 3 February 1967, coincidentally, the eighth anniversary of the death of Buddy Holly, Meek took a single barrelled shotgun and killed his landlady, Violet Shenton, who lived on the ground floor. He then returned to his studio, and shot himself. He was only thirty-seven years old.

# Index